What is Psychology?

What is Psychology?

Andrew M. Colman

Illustrated by Angela Chorley

Kogan Page, London

First published 1981 by Kogan Page Ltd,
120 Pentonville Road, London N1 9JN

Copyright © 1981 Andrew M. Colman
Illustrations © 1981 Angela Chorley

British Library Cataloguing in Publication Data

Colman, Andrew M
   What is psychology?
   1. Psychology
   I. Title
   150   BF121

   ISBN 0-85038-379-X
   ISBN 0-85038-413-3 Pbk

Printed in Great Britain by
The Anchor Press Ltd and bound by
Wm Brendon & Son Ltd,
both of Tiptree, Essex

Contents

Preface

This book is written primarily for seriously interested members of the general public and intending students of psychology. With such readers in mind, I have tried to convey a vivid and realistic picture of the subject as it is taught in colleges and universities, and of the activities of professional psychologists in their various fields of employment.

I have departed in two important ways from the usual conventions of brief introductoy books. The first is a matter of style. I have made copious use of concrete examples, given in sufficient detail to enable the reader to grasp them 'in the round' rather than merely to glimpse them in silhouette. These examples are intended to illustrate psychological research methods and findings and, more important, to provide a framework for discussing the ideas which lie behind them. The emphasis is always on discussion and explanation rather than bare description, and the reader is encouraged to take nothing for granted.

The second unusual feature of this book concerns its subject matter. I have included certain topics which are considered to be interesting and important by psychologists, and are dealt with in all undergraduate curricula, but are usually neglected or mentioned without explanation in books intended for non-psychologists. Experimental methods and statistics, for example, are discussed at some length because they are of central importance to most areas of psychology. These matters may bewilder many people and frighten intending students. Since brief, non-technical accounts are not readily available elsewhere, I have grasped the nettle and tried to present the essential ideas in a way which even the most non-mathematical readers may find palatable. I have included also a chapter on the history of psychology, in the belief that ideas are often easier to appreciate when they are viewed in historical perspective, and also because the development of psychology as a science is a fascinating subject in itself.

This is *not* a textbook. I have made no attempt to provide a balanced survey of the entire field of psychology, as any such attempt would be vain in a volume of this size, and would frustrate its essential aims. There are, in any event, a number of excellent comprehensive textbooks available, some of which are referred to in the pages which follow. I have concentrated instead on attempting to convey the flavour of the subject through a selection of its most important problems, methods, and findings. It is inevitable that some psychologists will not share my judgment of what is most important, and others will no doubt take issue with some of the views which are expressed in this book: psychology is a controversial subject. As a hint to reviewers, my own theoretical bias is cognitive and anti-positivist, and my research interests are mainly in the areas of social psychology and experimental aesthetics.

A number of friends and colleagues examined parts of an earlier draft of this book and made helpful comments. The following, in particular, brought grist to my mill: Felicity Dirmeik, Peter Freeman, Julia Gibbs, Gabriele Griffin, Ian Pountney, Jane Simpson, and Robert Thomson. Thanks are due also to Katy Carter of Kogan Page, who suggested a number of improvements, to Angela Chorley, who produced the captivating cartoons, and to Dorothy Brydges, who typed the manuscript.

A.M.C.
July 1980

1. Preliminary Discussion

O latest born and loveliest vision far
Of all Olympus' faded hierarchy

Keats: *Ode to Psyche*

Definitions

Among all the major branches of knowledge, psychology has the curious distinction of being the one which is most often mis-spelt. This is often harmless enough, but it can sometimes cause problems: a mis-spelt library request for a psychology book may turn up a volume devoted to phycology (the study of seaweed), psephology (the study of elections), physiology (the study of biological processes in plants and animals), or even psychography (spirit-writing).

The word *psychology* was coined about three centuries ago. It was formed by joining together two Greek words: the first is *psyche*, which originally meant *breath* and was later

extended to mean *spirit* or *soul* (since breath indicates that the spirit or soul is still in the body), and, more recently, *mind*; and the second is *logos*, originally meaning *word* and later *discourse* or *study*. The extended meanings of these Greek words suggest a natural definition of psychology as *the study of mind*, and in fact this definition was considered quite satisfactory in the past. Unfortunately, it has outlived its usefulness for a number of reasons. First, the contemplation of inner mental processes has been largely supplanted in modern psychology by more objective investigations of observable behaviour. Second, many of the things which psychologists study nowadays, such as brain mechanisms, are only indirectly related to mental processes, while others, for example instincts and reflexes, have next to nothing to do with the 'mind' as we normally understand the word. Third, a number of influential philosophers have challenged the view that the mind can be considered in isolation from behaviour; they have suggested that this is a 'category mistake' based on a fallacy of 'mind-body dualism', rather like that of a child watching a football match who asks: 'Who is the team spirit?'.

As a result of these developments, many contemporary psychologists prefer to define their discipline as *the study of behaviour* or *the science of behaviour*. But these definitions raise problems of their own. Although present-day psychologists base most of their conclusions on observations of behaviour, these conclusions often rest on inferences about the (unobservable) mental processes which underlie the behaviour; it is not always the behaviour *per se* which is of interest. Consider the following example: in studying the mental process we call dreaming, a psychologist may observe various objective events, such as rapid eye movements, deep muscular relaxation, characteristic patterns of brain waves, and (in male dreamers) penile erections. Psychologists know that these are signs of dreaming because people who are wakened while they are displaying them and asked to describe their mental states usually say that their dreams have been interrupted. But the significance of these signs lies in the fact that they indicate dreaming; they are of no great psychological interest in themselves.

Thus, to define psychology as the study of behaviour belies the fact that inferences are often made about mental processes which lie *behind* the behaviour; if we were to exclude mental processes altogether from the subject matter of psychology, the assumptions underlying such psychological investigations would collapse. More extreme cases can be cited of mental processes studied by psychologists which are not necessarily accompanied by *any* observable behaviour. Thinking, for example, has to be investigated in psychology by methods which are essentially indirect. Indirect methods are, of course, quite common in other fields of study as well. Astronomers investigate all manner of events in the heavens which, like mental processes, cannot be observed directly; their raw data are nowadays recorded largely by X-ray and radio receivers. But it would be silly to define astronomy as the study of the behaviour of these instruments. For the same reason, the various phenomena which are investigated in contemporary psychology are not easily squeezable into a definition based solely on behaviour.

The upshot of all this is that there is no generally accepted definition of psychology. But for those who have a deep longing for a definition, a suggestion can be offered which takes account of both behaviour and mental processes. For this purpose, mental processes may be divided into two categories: cognition (thinking and perceiving) and emotion (feeling). This leads to a definition of psychology as *the study of cognition, emotion, and behaviour.* There are problems associated with this definition as well, but nothing would be gained by prolonging the discussion since no entirely unobjectionable definition is possible. The truth of the matter is that definitions have very little practical usefulness. The only way of discovering the true nature of psychology is by examining specific examples of the kinds of things psychologists do and the kinds of things which they regard as falling outside the boundaries of their subject. Let us turn first to examples of the latter.

What Psychology is Not

Psychology is often confused with other academic

disciplines, practices, and professions. What follows is a discussion of some of the more common areas of confusion and the way in which these matters relate to psychology; it should help to clarify the boundaries of the discipline and to eliminate popular fallacies.

(a) Psychiatry. This is a branch of medicine devoted to the treatment of mental illnesses and other disorders in which psychological factors play a large part. A psychiatrist is a physician who has undergone a conventional medical training before specializing in psychiatry as an alternative to general practice, gynaecology, cardiology, or any other branch of medicine. As a medical specialist, a psychiatrist treats psychiatric patients and others who may be referred by general practitioners.

Psychologists receive no education in general medicine; their entire professional training is devoted to psychology. The work which most psychologists do is quite unrelated to abnormal behaviour or mental disorders. But the picture is complicated by the fact that a significant proportion of psychologists — about 15 per cent in Britain and a somewhat larger percentage in the United States — choose to follow professional careers in clinical psychology and practise psychotherapy alongside psychiatrists in mental hospitals and elsewhere. A patient receiving treatment for a mental disorder may be forgiven for not realizing that Dr Tweedledum (MB, ChB, DPM) is a medical doctor with a postgraduate Diploma in Psychological Medicine, in other words he is psychiatrist, while Dr Tweedledee (BSc, MSc, PhD) is a psychologist with a postgraduate Doctor of Philosophy degree in psychology. There may, however, be certain noticeable differences in their approach to treatment. Because of his training and background, Dr Tweedledee, the clinical psychologist, will not use purely medical forms of treatment, such as drugs, ECT (electro-convulsive therapy, or shock treatment), or psychosurgery.

(b) Psychoanalysis. This is a theory of mental structure and function — or more correctly a loosely connected set of theories and propositions — and an associated method of

psychotherapy initially based on the writings of the Viennese physician, Sigmund Freud (1856-1939). Its distinctive character arises from the emphasis which Freud placed on the role of unconscious mental processes and the various psychological mechanisms through which they are repressed. A familiar example of this is the Oedipus complex which, almost all psychoanalysts believe, arises in all pre-adolescent boys as a result of the repression of sexual desire for the mother and jealousy towards the father; the female counterpart of this is the Electra complex. (An application of psychoanalytic ideas to explain a common psychological disorder is outlined in Chapter 3 in connection with the case-history method of research.)

Psychoanalytic therapy relies on four techniques designed to provide insight into unconscious mental processes. The first is called *free association*. The analysand (subject of analysis) is placed in a relaxed and unthreatening atmosphere in which psychological defences are partly pacified, and is encouraged to report, and to continue to report, whatever

enters the mind, without hesitation or censorship, no matter how trivial or embarassing these thoughts may seem. The second technique is *dream analysis*. With the help of free association, the analyst guides the analysand in interpreting the symbolic meaning of the latter's dreams, in the belief that all latent dream content consists of unconscious wish-fulfillments. A third technique is the interpretation of *parapraxes*, or to use a more familiar term, *Freudian slips*. Slips of the tongue and other apparently accidental actions are thought by psychoanalysts to be no exception to the *law of psychic determinism* which asserts that all behaviour is the result of (possibly unconscious) psychological motives. Parapraxes are analysed for possible clues to repressed thoughts and desires in a manner similar to that used for dream interpretation. Finally, there is the technique of *transference,* in which the therapeutic relationship is used in a way which encourages the analysand to re-live aspects of past relationships with other people. A full psychoanalysis is a lengthy affair, consisting of several sessions per week over a period of years. During this time the analysand is supposed to gain some insight into the unconscious sources of the psychological problems, and this insight is thought to be beneficial in itself.

Since the early part of the twentieth century when Freud was practising, the psychoanalytic movement has been riven by doctrinal conflicts. The most influential of the present-day schools are based on the work of Anna Freud (Sigmund's daughter), Melanie Klein, Carl Gustav Jung, and Alfred Adler; their followers often refer to themselves as Freudian, Kleinian, Jungian, and Adlerian psychoanalysts respectively. The Jungian and Adlerian schools in particular represent radical departures — although along quite different lines — from the original theories and methods of Sigmund Freud.

The relationship between psychoanalysis, psychology, and psychiatry is very confusing. In the first place, psychoanalysts are not necessarily formally trained in either psychology or psychiatry; their essential training is achieved through undergoing a lengthy analysis themselves. Some psychologists and psychiatrists do, however, become psychoanalysts. A further source of confusion is that, particularly in continental Europe and the United States, many psychologists and psychiatrists who are not fully-fledged psychoanalysts are more or less psychoanalytically inclined in their approach. Nevertheless, a large proportion of American psychologists, and an even larger proportion in Britain, hold decidedly non-psychoanalytical or even anti-psychoanalytical views.

(c) Psychometrics. Roughly speaking, psychometrics is mental measurement or mental testing. It includes IQ, ability, and aptitude testing, and the use of psychological tests for the measurement of interests, attitudes, personality, and as a guide to the diagnosis of mental disorders. The modern approach to psychometrics began with the work of the French psychologist, Alfred Binet, who developed the first useful intelligence test in 1905. Psychometrics is an integral part of contemporary psychology, particularly of the branch of psychology which is concerned with differences between people. The great bulk of psychology, however, makes no use of psychometrics, since it is devoted to general psychological processes rather than individual differences. Members of the general public nevertheless often erroneously identify psychometrics with psychology as a whole, probably because the only direct contact which they have with psychology involves mental testing.

Many people are not only disturbed but also sceptical about the possibility of expressing their quintessentially human qualities, such as their intelligence or personality, in the form of mere numbers. Doubts of this kind usually reflect a misunderstanding of the logic of measurement, and they are on the whole not shared by psychologists. Criticisms of the uses to which psychometrics has sometimes been put, on the other hand, cannot be dismissed so easily. Many psychologists acknowledge that IQ tests in particular have often been abused for social and political purposes. The importation of Binet's IQ test into the United States, for example, led directly to the enactment of a number of sterilization laws aimed at 'subnormals', criminals, and other deviant groups, the refusal of entry into the country of refugees from the Nazi holocaust, and a wide range of discriminatory practices against ethnic minorities.

(d) Philosophy. A rough-and-ready definition of philosophy is *thought about thought.* Many of the problems which lay people assume to fall within the province of psychology are really philosophical problems. These are questions which cannot

be settled by any imaginable observations of human behaviour but which, by their very nature, must be dealt with by rational argument alone. This distinction is most easily illustrated with specific examples.

The psychology of perception is devoted to investigations of the way in which people use their sense organs in order to gain information about their environment. A major branch of philosophy, known as *epistemology*, is also concerned with investigating the nature and acquisition of knowledge about the world, but it centres on quite different types of questions. One of the central problems in epistemology, for example, is the *problem of induction,* first formulated by the Scottish philosopher David Hume in the eighteenth century. The problem is essentially this: how can we reach universal conclusions about the world on the basis of particular instances? What justification can be given for concluding that apples fall to the ground when released, when we know only that every apple we have *seen* behaves this way? If induction is not rationally justifiable, as most philosophers acknowledge, how is science possible? It is clear that we cannot solve this problem by studying human behaviour; it is an irreducibly philosophical problem which can be handled only by rational argument. (If you do not think it is a problem at all, you are mistaken; but do not be alarmed: philosophical problems often need to be thought about deeply before they are recognized as problems.)

Consider now the question of morality. Psychologists investigate the development and character of moral attitudes by studying the behaviour of children and adults, and useful insights emerge from this method of approach. But many problems relating to morality cannot be approached in this way: a second major branch of philosophy, known as *ethics*, centres on essentially philosophical problems of morality rather than the process of how we develop moral attitudes. For example, what are we to make of such an utterance as 'It is wrong to tell lies'? On the face of it, this is a factual statement, but a problem arises if we try to specify in what sense it can be considered true or false. Is it possible, either by logic or empirical evidence, to establish the truth or falsity of moral utterances? Or, as proponents of the doctrine of the *naturalistic fallacy* argue, is it an error to believe that they are in any sense statements of fact? Like the problem of induction mentioned earlier, and for the same reasons, this is a purely philosophical problem.

Two further sources of confusion of a rather trivial kind are worth brief mention. First, a small specialism in psychology, known as *philosophical psychology*, is devoted to the interface between the two disciplines. Second, many psychologists who have received no formal education in philosophy hold the degree of Doctor of Philosophy (PhD). The explanation is that, for historical reasons, the degree of PhD may be conferred on scholars following advanced postgraduate research in psychology, chemistry, Semitic languages, and most other academic subjects.

(e) Psychical Research. This field of investigation centres upon alleged 'paranormal' phenomena such as *extra-sensory perception* (ESP), or in simpler language, knowledge gained without the use of sense organs. Other areas of psychical research are devoted to *psychokinesis* (PK), or the movement of physical objects by mental effort alone, and to hauntings and other apparently paranormal happenings; but most psychical research to date has centred on ESP.

ESP may be divided into three classes. Perception of another person's thoughts is called *telepathy*, and extra-sensory perception of objects or events is called *clairvoyance*. When telepathy or clairvoyance relate to events in the future, they are called *precognition*. Psychical research has been devoted chiefly to determining whether or not any of these types of ESP occur. Popular writers on the subject frequently allege that the evidence is overwhelmingly in favour of ESP, and that members of the scientific establishment bury their heads in the sand and deliberately or unconsciously suppress this evidence because it challenges their cherished theories. But there are in fact several more substantial reasons for the scepticism of most establishment scientists towards ESP.

The first reason for scepticism is that positive results, when they have been reported, have to date usually suggested only very slight effects, and they have always turned out to be ephemeral: no one has yet uncovered a procedure which always or usually produces positive results when repeated. Second, many of the most dramatic demonstrations of ESP have been found to have been due either to inadequate experimental controls or — in numerous cases — to fraud or trickery on the part of the subjects or experimenters. The third and most fundamental source of scepticism is of a purely logical kind. Any conceivable example of ESP or any other psychical phenomenon may be caused by some unknown but perfectly normal process. If this process were revealed, the phenomenon could no longer be considered psychical. Eclipses, comets, volcanic eruptions, and plague epidemics were all once thought to have supernatural causes before they were properly understood as natural processes. No phenomenon could ever be decisively proved to be paranormal, because the possible normal explanations could never be exhaustively listed and refuted.

A small but active specialism in psychology, known as parapsychology, is devoted to investigations of psychical phenomena. The majority of parapsychologists tend to believe in the reality of such phenomena, but most other psychologists remain more or less sceptical. Only a very small proportion of research in psychology falls into the category of parapsychology.

(f) Sociology. This discipline is devoted to the study of the development and nature of entire societies and of the structures and processes within them. It was first recognized as an autonomous field of learning by the nineteenth century French philosopher, Auguste Comte. Its major present-day concerns can be traced largely to the writings of three influential social theorists. Karl Marx (1818-83) was the first to draw attention to the central importance of class conflict as a factor in the functioning and change of societies; he argued that economic relations and modes of production were the fundamental bases of society, determining both action and ideology. Emile Durkheim (1858-1917) focussed attention on social cohesion, or solidarity; he analysed social

change in terms of the replacement of isolated social hierarchies by the complex and interdependent social relations of modern society, arguing that the rate of suicide increases as a function of the disintegration of social norms (*anomie*). He saw 'collective conscience' — the system of values and customs governing social behaviour — as the foundation of all religion and the central source of social stability. Max Weber's (1864-1920) major concern was with rationality; economics and law were analysed by him in terms of rational human action, and religion was seen as a model of non-rational action; types of authority and bureaucracy were also classified by Weber partly according to this distinction.

There is evidently considerable overlap between the concerns of sociologists and psychologists, but the focus of attention is quite different. Sociologists are interested in peoples' thoughts, perceptions, feelings, and behaviour, but their objects of investigation are large aggregates of people, while psychologists investigate these things at the level of the individual. There is also an important difference between the two disciplines in methodology; empirical observations are often used by psychologists to test theories by means of controlled experiments, while sociologists use them only descriptively or illustratively since controlled experiments in sociology are not feasible.

Social psychology forms a part of many undergraduate degree courses in sociology. The approach to social psychology adopted by most sociologists is, however, distinctly sociological in flavour compared with that of a typical social psychologist with a purely psychological background.

Discovering Psychology

The formal definitions given at the beginning of this chapter provide one kind of answer to the question 'What is psychology?', but they convey scarcely anything of the flavour of the discipline. The discussion about what psychology is *not* will have inoculated the reader against some of the most flagrant misrepresentations which abound in novels, films, popular magazines, and everyday conversations, and which cause professional psychologists to wince. But in order to gain anything approaching a true understanding, it is necessary to remove the veil and examine some of the fine detail of the discipline from close range. There is no short cut on the path to sound knowledge.

The best way of making a close examination of psychology is by enrolling for a degree course at a reputable institution of higher learning. For obvious reasons, this line of approach is not available to many of those who wish to know something about psychology. Furthermore, people who are considering enrolling for such courses are often sensible enough to seek information about the subject before committing themselves to a long and often expensive venture into higher education.

Various other possibilities present themselves. The needs of some people are adequately served by the short introductory courses in psychology which many adult education centres provide through the medium of evening classes or summer schools. These courses are sometimes quite informative and enjoyable, but the level at which the subject is presented is usually extremely elementary and somewhat popularized, and the range of topics covered is typically severely restricted. Another possibility is to consult a number of introductory psychology textbooks, which can usually be obtained quite easily through public libraries. But surveys conducted by psychologists have shown that such textbooks tend to present a very biased and misleading view of the subject, and they are frequently quite out of date. A brave way of attempting to find out about psychology is by consulting the primary sources, namely the technical papers through which psychologists report their research findings in the scholarly journals which are available in most university libraries. Unfortunately, a novice would find this exercise quite unrewarding, because the technical articles presuppose a knowledge of basic concepts and statistical techniques without which they are all but unintelligible.

For the reader who has no previous acquaintance with psychology, Chapter 2 should prove particularly useful in providing a close-up view of some of the nuts and bolts of the discipline. It contains a selection from a wide range of concrete examples of psychological research of the kind dealt with in most degree courses in psychology. I have made no attempt to conceal the fact that parts of psychology *are* difficult, or to patronize the reader; I assume that people who choose to read this book are serious in their desire to learn what psychology is like. All of the examples are, however, explained in plain language and no specialized knowledge is assumed, so that anyone who reads the examples attentively will be able to understand the fundamental ideas in each case. The examples are presented in the form of a self-assessment quiz. After completing the quiz and studying the answers carefully, the reader will no longer be entirely in the dark.

Further Reading

The problem of defining psychology is a sterile one and is probably not worth pursuing in depth. The suggestion that mental events cannot be considered in isolation from behaviour, and the concept of the category mistake, were first proposed by G. Ryle in his readable and influential (though controversial) book, *The Concept of Mind* (London: Hutchinson, 1949). Brief outlines of psychiatry, psycho-analysis, psychometrics, philosophy, psychical research, and sociology, written by leading authorities in each case, and including some well-chosen bibliographies, are given in *The Fontana Dictionary of Modern Thought*, edited by A. Bullock and O. Stallybrass (London: Fontana, 1977). Introductory psychology textbooks which provide fairly comprehensive surveys include Hilgard, E. R., Atkinson, R. L., and Atkinson, R. C., *Introduction to Psychology*, 7th ed. (New York: Harcourt Brace Jovanovich, 1979); and Davies, A. T., Sluckin, W., Davies, D. R., Reason, J. T., Thomson, R., and Colman, A. M., *Introducing Psychology* (Harmondsworth: Penguin, 1981).

2. Psychology and Common Sense: A Self-assessment Quiz

The main purpose of this chapter is to present a wide range of examples illustrating the kinds of things research psychologists do. This is the best way — perhaps the only way — of imparting a clear idea of the nature and scope of the discipline. Abstract discussions *about* psychology have therefore been deferred to later chapters, to be tackled after the appetite has first been whetted with an *hors d'oeuvre* of concrete examples. The examples are presented in the form of a series of questions and answers, partly to highlight the fact that psychology is a problem-solving activity. While there may be a grain of truth in the belief that psychologists love giving people tests, it is certainly true that many people love *taking* tests. Quiz addicts may therefore find this chapter entertaining as well as informative.

One of George Bernard Shaw's admirers once asked him: 'Can you play the violin?' 'I don't know,' replied Shaw, 'I've never tried.' If someone were to make the same joke about understanding human behaviour rather than playing the violin, it would not raise many laughs. The fact is that everyone tries to understand human behaviour; everyone is an amateur psychologist. It is obvious that violin playing requires specialized knowledge and training, but many people believe that psychology is indeed nothing but common sense. Those without any specialized knowledge or training in the subject should therefore find the quiz especially challenging and instructive.

The reader is strongly urged to try to answer each of the questions before turning to the explanations. This advice is based upon sound psychological principles: for even if you get all the answers wrong, your interest in the underlying problems will be aroused, and you will be much more impressed by the right answers when you meet them.

Instructions. Work through the questions in the order given. Note that in some cases more than one of the suggested alternatives are correct, and in other cases all the alternatives are wrong. Answers and detailed explanations follow the questions. Keep a careful record of your answers on a separate sheet of paper. An interpretation of scores is given at the end of the chapter.

Questions

1. Dreams often seem to be quite prolonged affairs. But Shakespeare apparently believed that they come and go in an instant. In *A Midsummer Night's Dream* (I.i), Lysander talks about 'true love' and compares it to a dream in order to emphasize how 'brief' or 'momentary' it is. 'The course of true love never did run smooth,' declares Lysander; it is 'Swift as a shadow, short as any dream'. How long does a typical dream really last: (a) a fraction of a second; (b) a few seconds; (c) a minute or two; (d) many minutes; (e) several hours? Take a bonus point for correctly answering the following question about yourself: Do you dream: (f) hardly ever or never; (g) approximately once every few nights; (h) approximately once a night; (i) several times every night?

2. Nathaniel was exhausted from overwork. He slumped into bed and fell into a deep sleep. After a while he began to twist and turn and mutter 'Please....please....' and his wife, who was lying beside him, found this rather alarming. She wondered whether he was about to start sleep-walking, and whether she ought to wake him up in case he was having a nightmare. Do sleep-walking and sleep-talking occur: (a) mostly during nightmares; (b) mostly during ordinary dreams; (c) neither?

3. This is a straightforward question about the wiring of the human nervous system. Attached to the retina of each eye are nerves which respond to light and transmit visual

23

information to the brain. Are all the nerve fibres from the left eye connected to: (a) the left half of the brain; (b) the right half of the brain; (c) the centre of the brain (the pineal gland)? Take a bonus point if you can describe more or less correctly the pathways to the brain of both the touch-sensitive nerves in the skin, and the nerves which respond to sound vibrations in the ear.

4. John grew restless and wandered into the kitchen where his mother was baking a cake for his ninth birthday. On the kitchen table were two unopened bottles of milk. John watched while his mother opened one of the bottles and poured the contents into a large glass bowl. His eyes roved from the remaining bottle of milk to the bowl and back

again. His mother was suddenly reminded of something she had read in a psychology textbook. 'Tell me, clever boy,' she said, 'is there more milk in the bottle or in the bowl?' Is John likely to have thought that: (a) the bottle contained more milk; (b) the bowl contained more milk; (c) the bottle and the bowl contained the same amount of milk?

5. Chapter 9 of the *Gospel According to Saint John* is devoted entirely to an episode in which Jesus restored the sight of a man 'which was blind from his birth'. According to a briefer account in *Mark* (8: 22-6), Jesus spat on the blind man's eyes, touched them with his hands, and asked him whether he could see. 'And he looked up, and said, I see men as trees, walking.' Jesus was evidently not entirely satisfied: he touched the man's eyes once again. This time 'he was

restored, and saw every man clearly'.

In more recent times, people born blind have sometimes had their sight restored late in life by surgical rather than miraculous methods. During the first few days after the bandages are removed, do such people: (a) see nothing at all; (b) see only a blur; (c) see only vague shapes moving about, like the blind man in the Bible following Jesus's first attempt; (d) recognize familiar objects without touching them; (e) see everything clearly, like the man in the Bible following Jesus's second attempt; (f) see everything upside down?

6. This question has a sting in its tail. Hans, the butler, noticed that the light bulb which hung in the centre of the main drawing-room needed replacing. He climbed up a step-ladder until the light bulb was at eye-level. His head and shoulders were completely surrounded by a large drum-shaped parchment lampshade which hung from the light fitting. As he tried to unscrew the faulty bulb, the lampshade began to rotate around him to the right. At that moment Hans froze. He was suddenly aware of a mysterious loud buzzing noise. What Hans did not know was that a

large bee was hovering just outside the rotating lampshade a short distance in front of his nose. From which direction do you suppose Hans thought the sound was coming: (a) from in front; (b) from behind; (c) from overhead; (d) from the left; (e) from the right? Take a bonus point if you can give the correct reason for the answer.

7. You may be pleased to learn, especially if you consider yourself to be tone deaf, that under ideal conditions you can probably just hear the difference in pitch between a musical tone of 1000 hertz (cycles per second) and one of 1003 hertz. If the first tone were 2000 hertz, ie an octave higher than before, which (if any) of the following tones would you be able to distinguish from it: (a) 2001 hertz; (b) 2002 hertz; (c) 2003 hertz; (d) 2004 hertz; (e) 2005 hertz?

Take a bonus point for correctly answering this question: Under ideal conditions, which (if any) of the following light intensities would seem noticeably brighter than one of 1000 watts: (f) 1001 watts; (g) 1002 watts; (h) 1003 watts; (i) 1006 watts; (j) 1012 watts; (k) 1018 watts; (l) 1024 watts?

8. Gustav was trying to read a difficult psychology book by the light of a single candle in order to save electricity (he was a very eccentric old man). His eyes began to hurt, and he decided that he needed to double the brightness of the light. How many further candles would have to be lit to make Gustav think that the brightness had been doubled: (a) 1; (b) 2; (c) 3; (d) 4; (e) 5; (f) 6; (g) 7; (h) 8; (i) 9; (j) 10? Now consider the following closely related problem.

Smith was a creative chef. He prepared two sauces, A and B, according to the same recipe except for the amount of salt used in each. 'This one is delicious,' said one of the dinner guests, pointing to Sauce B; 'could you give me the recipe, Smith?' 'Oh dear,' said Smith, 'I can't remember how much salt went into that one.' The dinner guests carefully compared the two sauces for saltiness. The general consensus of opinion was that Sauce B tasted twice as salty as Sauce A. 'Ah, well,' said Smith, 'I remember putting a quarter of a teaspoon of salt in Sauce A, so I suppose I must have put half a teaspoon in Sauce B.' One of the dinner guests was a competent psychologist. He thought for a moment and then announced that Sauce B contained: (k) less than half a teaspoon of salt; (l) more than half a teaspoon of salt; (m) exactly half a teaspoon of salt?

Take a bonus point for correctly stating the general law which underlies both problems.

9. 'A musical note' said the physics teacher, moving his hand through the air in a graceful ripple, 'is a sound wave. The A above middle C, for example, is a wave of 440 hertz or cycles per second. If we increase the amplitude of this wave, the intensity of the sound increases. Can anyone tell me how this would affect the sound of our 440-hertz note?' Which of the following replies given by the children is correct: (a) it sounds louder and slightly lower in pitch; (b) it sounds louder and slightly higher in pitch; (c) it sound louder but the same pitch; (d) it sounds softer but the same pitch?

10. What irritated Susan most about Richard was his over-confidence: he never admitted that he was wrong about anything. After thumbing through a psychology textbook, Susan chose two ordinary tin cans from the kitchen. One of the cans was much bigger than the other. She put half a pound of butter inside each of them and replaced their lids. 'Rich darling,' she said, 'I've got a problem. Are you good at judging weights?' 'I am rather,' replied Richard. 'I can tell you've put on a pound or two,' he added, lifting Susan off the ground. Susan showed him the tin cans. 'I'm sure there's something wrong with the kitchen scales' she lied. 'Which can do you think is heavier? Take your time feeling them.' Which of the following replies is Richard likely to have given: (a) the smaller can feels very slightly heavier; (b) the smaller can feels much heavier; (c) the larger can feels very slightly heavier; (d) the larger can feels much heavier; (e) neither can feels noticeably heavier than the other?

11. Edwin put an ordinary black-and-white film into his camera, fitted a green filter over the lens, and photographed a bowl of fruit. He made a black-and-white transparency and projected the image on to a screen with a slide projector. The projected image consisted of various shades of grey.

Edwina photographed the same bowl of fruit from the same position, also on black-and-white film. She used a red filter over the camera lens, however, and also over the lens of the slide projector used to display the black-and-white transparency. This image consisted of various shades of pink.

Supposing the two projected images were superimposed on each other, how would the composite image appear: (a) entirely in shades of grey; (b) entirely in shades of pink; (c) partly in shades of grey and partly in shades of pink; (d) in full natural colour, with red strawberries, green apples, blue plums, yellow bananas etc?

12. 'We'll have an ongoing strike situation on our hands unless we manage to persuade the work-force that we simply can't afford to meet their ridiculous pay demand' said the company chairman. 'I think Leon should go outside and explain the scenario to them.' Leon lowered his eyes. 'I don't fancy that idea much,' he said. 'I personally think the pay demand is quite reasonable.' 'My dear chap,' said the chairman, '*you* don't have to believe what you say; only *they* have got to believe it. And, I need hardly say, we'll pay you for your cooperation in this matter.' After the chairman had handed him a cheque, Leon went out and succeeded in persuading the assembled workers to withdraw their pay demand. Would you expect Leon's personal attitude towards the pay demand, when he had spoken out against it, to become (a) less favourable; (b) more favourable? Take a bonus point for correctly predicting whether there would probably be a greater change in his attitude: (c) if he was paid a small amount; (d) if he was paid a large amount.

13. Hermann devised a novel method of making money. He advertized a course in memory training. His method of memory training was based on a pack of 20 cards, each of which had a nonsense syllable (DAX, FUB, etc) typed on it. Each person who enrolled for the course was first required to memorize the 20 nonsense syllables. He or she was allowed to run through the pack once, examining each card for a few seconds, and was then asked to write down as many of the nonsense syllables as could be remembered. This procedure was repeated several times until all 20 items were correctly recalled. After 24 hours, Hermann instructed the trainee once again to write down as many of the nonsense syllables

as could be remembered. On this final test, do you suppose that: (a) quick learners remembered more items than slow learners; (b) people with good memories remembered more items than those with poor memories; (c) most people remembered approximately the same number of items? Take a bonus point for correctly answering this question: Suppose Hermann had used material which is easier to learn than nonsense syllables, such as simple words (HOUSE, CHAIR, etc). Do you suppose that on average: (d) more items would have been remembered; (e) fewer items would have been remembered; (f) approximately the same number of items would have been remembered?

14. This is a question about little furry animals. Burrhus put one of the albino rats which he kept as pets into a box. To avoid the bother of feeding, the box was fitted with a lever which released a food pellet whenever it was pressed by the rat. After 150 lever-presses, Burrhus noticed that the rat had acquired the habit of pressing the lever to get its reward; it continued to press the lever even though the food pellets were no longer delivered.

Burrhus repeated this procedure with a second rat. He was running short of food pellets, however, so he set his machine to deliver them on average once for every five lever-presses. He continued as before until the rat had pressed the lever 150 times. Once again he found that the rat had acquired a habit which persisted when the pellets of food were no longer delivered.

Do you suppose that after this training: (a) the first rat displayed the habit for longer than the second rat; (b) the second rat displayed the habit for longer than the first rat; (c) both rats displayed the habit for approximately the same length of time; (d) the first rat displayed neurotic behaviour; (e) the second rat displayed neurotic behaviour; (f) both rats displayed neurotic behaviour?

15. The influential philosopher Friedrich Nietzsche suffered from insanity and general ill-health for many years. The great physicist Albert Einstein, on the other hand, was perfectly sane and enjoyed good health throughout most of

his three score years and sixteen. Are exceptionally intelligent people in general: (a) less physically and mentally healthy than others; (b) more physically and mentally healthy than others; (c) similar to others in physical and mental health; (d) less mentally healthy but similar to others in physical health; (e) less physically healthy but similar to others in mental health?

16. This question touches on the somewhat delicate issue of social class and the even more delicate issue of mental illness. Do you suppose that schizophrenia, the most common of serious mental illnesses in Western industrial societies, is: (a) more common among unskilled working-class people than among the upper-middle class; (b) more common among upper-middle class people than among unskilled workers; (c) approximately equally common in all social classes? Take a bonus point if you can correctly answer the same question with respect to the mental illness known as childhood autism, which resembles schizophrenia in many respects.

17. Most people have heard about the psychological disorder, illustrated in Robert Louis Stevenson's *Dr Jekyll and Mr Hyde*, in which an individual alternates between two or more distinct personality types. Does this disorder fall into the category of: (a) neurosis; (b) schizophrenia; (c) manic-depressive psychosis?

18. A group of friends decided to spend some money placing bets on a series of horse races. Before each race they wrote down their private decisions regarding the bet which should be placed. The group then assembled to discuss their individual opinions and to arrive at a group decision. In each case, the most cautious decision was not to place any bet, a more risky decision was to place a small bet on a horse with favourable odds of winning, and a very risky decision was to place a large bet on an 'outsider'. Are the group decisions in each case likely to have been: (a) more cautious; (b) more risky; (c) neither more cautious nor more risky than the average of the individual decisions?

19. This question is designed to test your knowledge of sex. Which (if any) of the following do you suppose are common to all known human societies: (a) prohibition of sex between certain close relatives; (b) knowledge of the connection between sexual intercourse and pregnancy; (c) general disapproval of homosexuality?

20. A seven-member committee was set up to decide which of three candidates, Adams, Brown, or Carter, to appoint to a vacant post. Each committee member had a definite order of preference, and after a long discussion it became clear that a unanimous decision could not be reached, so they decided to take a vote. Three committee members voted for Adams, two voted for Brown, and two voted for Carter. Is it possible that a majority of the committee members preferred: (a) Brown to Carter; (b) Brown to Adams; (c) Carter to Adams?

Answers and Explanations

1 (d, i). Score one point for each correct answer. A typical dream lasts for about 20 minutes, and all people dream several times every night spent sleeping. You may believe that you dream much less than this, because most dreams are forgotten; we normally remember only fragments of dreams which occur shortly before waking.

These research findings arose from the accidental discovery in the early 1950s of a reliable behavioural indicator of dreaming. A graduate student in the United States, Eugene Aserinsky, noticed rapid eye movements occurring behind the closed eyelids of sleeping infants. By waking people during rapid eye movement sleep (REM sleep) and periods without rapid eye movements (NREM sleep), William Dement and Nathaniel Kleitman were later able to establish that this is a fairly reliable indicator of dreaming. Some dreamlike mental activity is now known to occur occasionally during NREM sleep, but it differs in various ways from REM dreams: it more often centres upon commonplace events, it contains relatively little symbolic elaboration, and it is generally less bizarre than a full-blown dream.

Electroencephalogram (EEG or brain-wave) studies have uncovered characteristically different patterns of electrical activity in the brain during REM and NREM sleep. Roughly speaking, the EEG patterns associated with REM sleep resemble those of people who are awake rather than those of people who are in deeper slow-wave sleep. Nevertheless, people are most difficult to awaken from REM sleep. For these reasons, some psychologists refer to REM sleep as *paradoxical sleep.*

All people who have been investigated since the early 1950s, including those who claim that they never dream, have shown several dreaming episodes every night spent sleeping. Adults spend approximately 20 per cent of the night dreaming, and infants and young children spend considerably more time — approximately 50 per cent — in this state. The normal pattern in adults is made up of four or five dreaming episodes which occur at roughly 90-minute intervals. These episodes grow longer towards morning; the first may continue for five or ten minutes and the last for half an hour or more. Contrary to popular belief, dreams usually occupy approximately the same amount of time as the events dreamed about; a dream about a five-minute bus-ride lasts for roughly five minutes.

There is some indirect evidence which suggests that REM sleep in general, or dreaming in particular, serves an important biological function. In several experiments, subjects have been deprived of REM sleep by being wakened whenever a REM episode begins, and then allowed to go back to sleep. Compared with people who had been deprived of equal amounts of NREM sleep, these subjects later compensated for the lost REM sleep by dreaming a great deal more than usual.

Reference: Cohen, D. B. *Sleep and Dreaming: Origins, Nature and Functions.* Oxford: Pergamon, 1979.

2 (c). Score one point. Contrary to the beliefs of movie-makers, sleep-talking and sleep-walking do not normally occur during nightmares or dreams. They usually occur

during NREM sleep (see the answer to Question 1).

During REM sleep, a person's mind may be very active as he dreams about talking, running, playing games and the like, but his body remains in a state of immobility bordering on paralysis, apart from eye movements and occasional twitches. A special brain mechanism has been found which comes into operation during REM sleep to inhibit bodily activity by blocking nerve impulses to the muscles. The function of this mechanism is evidently to prevent the dreamer from acting out his dreams; when this brain mechanism was deliberately destroyed in experiments on cats, the animals ran about, hissed, and spat during REM episodes, although they were fast asleep. This mechanism can be partly counteracted in some humans without surgery by means of hypnosis. A good hypnotic subject may be given the suggestion under hypnosis that he will describe his dreams the following night, while they are actually occurring, without waking up. In the morning, if he remembers the dream at all, it will usually be only a fragmentary and distorted version of the dream which he described while it occurred.

Reference: Hartmann, E. L. *The Functions of Sleep.* New Haven: Yale University Press, 1973.

3. Score one point for realizing that none of the alternatives given in this tricky question is correct, and a further point for describing the pathways for touch and hearing more or less correctly (see below).

The retina of each eye is divided into two halves. The lens of the eye focusses light from the centre of the visual field — the point on which the gaze is fixed — on to the *fovea* in the middle of the retina. Light from the left visual field — the area to the left of the point on which the gaze is centred — falls on the right halves of both retinas. Conversely, light from the right visual field falls on the left halves of both retinas.

The nerve fibres from *one half* of each retina cross to the opposite side of the brain; the rest are connected to the corresponding hemisphere. The crossed fibres are the ones attached to the inner halves of the retinas (the halves located nearer the bridge of the nose); the uncrossed fibres come from the outer halves of the retinas.

From the action of the lenses and the peculiar wiring of the human visual system, the following can be deduced. All the information from the left visual field — which is recorded by the inner half of the retina of the left eye and the outer half of the retina of the right eye — ends up in the right hemisphere of the brain. Information from the right visual field is transmitted by both eyes to the left hemisphere of the brain. To put it another way, all the information from the left or right of the visual field is carried by the nerve fibres to the opposite side of the brain.

This is dramatically illustrated in cases of damage to the brain in the area where the nerve fibres from the eyes terminate. The brain area in question is located at the back of the head and is known as the *visual cortex*. It is split between the two hemispheres. People whose right visual cortex is damaged by accident or disease lose vision in both eyes for the left half of the visual field. People with left visual cortex damage are blind in the right visual field. An astonishing feature of this form of semi-blindness is that it often goes unnoticed: people suffering from such damage are typically unaware for months or years that they are completely lacking vision for half the visual field. Though unable to see anything to the right (or left) of the point on which their gaze is fixed, they do not seem to notice that anything is missing. They may tend to bump into pieces of furniture and fail to notice things which other people call attention to, but they cannot easily pinpoint the nature of their disability.

The *partial decussation* (partial crossing over) of the visual nerve fibres in humans was first recognized by Isaac Newton in 1704. It raises the interesting question: What is the function of such a seemingly complicated system? Partial decussation has been found in certain non-human animals as well, but in birds and fishes the fibres are completely crossed. In mammals, the percentage of uncrossed fibres is related to the amount of overlap in the visual fields of the two eyes. As animals evolved with eyes more to the front of the head than to the side, the percentage of uncrossed fibres increased. The rabbit, for example, has only a tiny overlap of visual fields, and a correspondingly small percentage of uncrossed fibres; in humans, there is a large overlap of visual fields, and half the fibres are uncrossed. The evolution of partial decussation is thus closely associated with the evolution of overlapping visual fields. This suggests a clue to its function.

The clue concerns stereoscopic vision, which must have proved to be a remarkably useful device when tree-dwelling predatory animals evolved. Overlapping visual fields provide an extremely accurate method of stereoscopic depth perception. The distance of an object can be finely judged by the degree to which its images on the retinas differ from each other. Since each eye records the visual field from a slightly different vantage point, the retinal images are not quite identical: the closer an object is to the eyes, the greater is the *binocular parallax* or disparity between the two images. In order for the two images to be compared with each other, however, it is necessary for the visual information from both eyes to be transmitted to a single area of the brain. The seventeenth century French philosopher René Descartes thought that the information from both eyes converges on the pineal gland in the centre of the brain. Subsequent research, however, revealed that the pineal gland plays no such role; its true function is to secrete hormones into the blood (it is an endocrine gland). During the nineteenth century, the German physiologist Hermann von Helmholtz suggested that there must nevertheless be some area in the brain in which the information from the two eyes is compared. He called this the 'Cyclopean eye', alluding to the Cyclops in Greek mythology which had an eye in the middle of its forehead.

In 1959, David Hubel and Torsten Wiesel of Harvard University discovered that the visual cortex contains cells which respond to impulses received from both eyes. The Cyclopean eye had at last been discovered. It is these cells in the visual cortex which enable people and certain other animals to locate objects in space by comparing the images received by the two eyes in the region where the visual fields overlap. This method of depth perception is not available to animals whose visual fields do not overlap and whose visual pathways are completely crossed, since in these animals the information from the two eyes is transmitted to opposite sides of the brain. It is possible only if information from corresponding points of the visual field is fed to single cells in the visual cortex. This is elegantly achieved by means of partial decussation: information from points in the left visual field is received by both eyes and is transmitted to corresponding cells in the right visual cortex where any disparities can be immediately detected by cells which are wired to respond to different degrees of disparity. Both views of the right visual field are similarly transmitted to corresponding cells in the left visual cortex.

The auditory system is also partly crossed. This is necessary for purposes of sound localization (see the answer to Question 6). In the case of hearing, however, the crossed connections are somewhat stronger than the uncrossed ones. The nerve pathways associated with touch and movement, for their part, are almost completely crossed. Sensations of touch and bodily movements are served almost entirely by the opposite hemispheres of the brain. There is, of course, no obvious function which would be fulfilled by partial decussation in this case.

Reference: Pettigrew, J. D. The neurophysiology of binocular vision. *Scientific American*, 1972, **227**(2), 84-95.

4 (c). Score one point. John is very likely to have thought that the bottle and the bowl contained the same amount of milk. It was a trick question, since a child a few years younger would probably have thought that the bottle contained more milk. The great majority of children in Western industrial societies, however, have mastered the *conservation of substance* by the time they are nearly nine years old. The experiment and the concept of conservation derive from the work of the Swiss psychologist, Jean Piaget (1896-1980).

The relevant part of Piaget's theory of intellectual

development concerns the *pre-operational* stage of development. An important feature of this stage is what Piaget calls *centration* or, roughly speaking, a tendency to focus attention on only one aspect of a problem at a time. One consequence of this is the pre-operational child's inability to solve problems involving conservation.

Suppose, for example, a pre-operational child is shown a row of egg-cups each containing an egg. If the eggs are removed and spread out in a longer row than the row of egg-cups, the child will centre on the different lengths of the rows, ignoring differences in density (which are harder to grasp), and conclude that there are more eggs than egg-cups. This reveals a failure to conserve number. Inability to conserve substance is illustrated by the experiment described in the question. Tests for conservation of mass and volume traditionally make use of balls of plasticine of different shapes but containing the same amount of matter which are weighed in a balance or immersed in water.

The development of conservation, whether of number, substance, mass, or volume, proceeds through three phases. In the experiment described in the question, for example, the child first centres on the height of the milk, ignoring the narrowness of the bottle compared with the bowl, and concludes that the bottle contains more milk. During the second phase, the child vacillates: sometimes the correct answer is given and sometimes centration takes hold. The final phase is characterized by complete mastery of conservation with complete *decentration:* the child has no difficulty taking more than one factor into account simultaneously.

The same sequence of development has been found in Swiss, English, American, and Canadian children, and even those from very different cultures in Africa, Asia, and Latin America. The various different types of conservation have generally been found to appear in the same order: first number and substance, then mass, and finally volume. The typical ages at which these abilities are mastered, however, vary slightly from one culture to the next. Piaget found conservation of number and substance to be mastered typically by seven or eight years of age, but present-day English and American children usually reach this stage slightly earlier. The child referred to in the question is very likely indeed to have mastered conservation of substance, since he is nearly nine years old.

Reference: Piaget, J. and Inhelder, B. *The Psychology of the Child*, translated by H. Weaver. London: Routledge and Kegan Paul, 1969.

5 (d). Score one point. People whose blindness is cured late in life are able to recognize familiar objects without touching them. This question has been debated since the seventeenth century, but it was not convincingly solved until careful psychological investigations were made in the 1960s and 1970s.

In his *Essay Concerning Human Understanding* published in 1690, the philosopher John Locke speculated at some length about what the world would look like to a person who suddenly acquired the gift of sight late in life. He realized that this experiment of nature might provide a critical test of his empiricist ideas (see Chapter 5). He took the view that such a person would not at first be able to distinguish even familiar objects by sight alone. To explain his reasons for this belief, he quoted a letter from his friend, 'the learned and worthy Mr Molineux', who thought that even a globe and a cube would at first be indistinguishable to such a person by sight alone: 'For, though he has obtained the experience of how a globe, how a cube affects his touch, yet he has not yet obtained the experience that what affects his touch so or so must affect his sight so or so' (Bk. 2, Ch. 9, Sect. 8).

Congenital blindness is, fortunately for humanity at large but unfortunately for psychologists interested in the role of experience in vision, extremely rare. When the condition is curable, it is even rarer to find it remaining untreated for more than a few years. It should be pointed out that total blindness — absolute insensitivity to light — has never been successfully cured. The cases of congenital blindness which have been successfully treated are those in which cataracts of the lens or opacity of the cornea were present in both eyes. In all these cases the retinas were functioning normally, and the patients were presumably aware of light and darkness to some extent. But they were effectively blind in so far as they could not perceive the outlines of objects.

In 1932, Marius von Senden searched through the world's medical literature and found reports of 66 cases of blindness cured late in life. This evidence seemed to suggest that the patients could not at first recognize or name any common objects, determine the sizes of objects, count the number of objects in a group, or evaluate their distance by sight alone. But none of the cases, the most recent of which had been reported in 1904, was carefully examined or properly tested, and the reports are all unsatisfactory and unreliable for a variety of reasons.

In 1963, the British psychologists Richard Gregory and Jean Wallace reported the first detailed and rigorous examination of recovery from blindness. The patient was a 52 year old man whose sight had recently been restored through surgery. He had been blind since he was less than a year old. The examination of this man, referred to as S.B., revealed a number of surprising facts.

There is little doubt that S.B. could recognize familiar objects, including chairs, beds, and tables, almost immediately, and certainly within hours of the removal of his bandages. It is clear that he could recognize things by sight without touching them. He could tell the time from a large clock on the wall. He could distinguish motor cars, lorries, and buses at a distance by looking at them through a window. He was able to draw a recognizable picture of a hammer, an object which he had never seen. Most impressively of all, he could read printed capital letters on the cover of a magazine. He was, of course, familiar with the shape of capital letters: blind people are normally taught to read them by touch since they are often embossed on name plates. But, using Mr Molineux's argument, S.B. had not had any opportunity to learn the connection between the way capital letters look and feel, since there were no embossed letters in the hospital ward where he had been confined since his operation. S.B. was occasionally surprised by what he saw. He was disappointed by the drabness of most colours. He was startled by the appearance of the crescent moon: he had apparently expected it to assume the shape of a slice of cake! On the other hand, he found his wife 'just as bonny as I thought she would be'.

In 1971, Alberto Valvo reported evidence in Rome of a number of further cases. This evidence confirmed the findings of Gregory and Wallace on important details. In particular, Valvo confirmed that capital letters, previously learned by touch, could immediately be recognized through vision alone by these patients. The question posed by John Locke in 1690 seems now to be more or less settled, and the conclusions do not confirm Locke's predictions.

It is perhaps worth mentioning a surprising psychological finding on which the older and the more recent evidence agrees entirely. It seems that, far from being overjoyed by the discovery of the wonderful world of vision, people whose blindness is cured late in life tend to become depressed. This was certainly true of S.B., who apparently committed suicide soon after the operation, and there are numerous similar examples in von Senden's account. One of von Senden's cases, originally reported by the French physician Franz Anton Mesmer in 1777, is typical. This woman wrote as follows: 'How comes it that I now find myself less happy than before? Everything that I see causes me a disagreeable emotion. Oh, I was much more at ease in my blindness'. One can only speculate about the reasons for this curious psychological reaction so often found in those whose blindness is cured.

Reference: Gregory, R.L. *Concepts and Mechanisms of Perception* (Ch. 3). London: Duckworth, 1974.

6 (c). Score one point for the correct answer and one for the correct explanation (see below). The sound would have seemed to come from overhead, but to explain this curious fact it is necessary first to explain how we normally sense the direction of sounds.

For a low-pitched sound, localization is achieved principally by detecting the phase difference in the time at which the peaks of the sound wave reach the two ears; the peaks take fractionally longer to reach the ear furthest from the sound source. In an open area with no reflecting surfaces, or in a laboratory simulation of this situation using earphones, low-pitched sounds can be located to within 10 degrees. This requires the detection of an amazingly small time difference between the movements of the two ear-drums of less than one ten-thousandth of a second.

Localization of high-frequency sounds also requires binaural hearing, but in this case differences in intensity rather than phase are detected. Because the wavelength of a high-pitched tone is smaller than the diameter of the head, a sonic shadow is formed on the side furthest from the sound source; the more distant ear therefore receives a less intense signal than the other. This second method of localization is used for sounds above about 1000 hertz or cycles per second, that is about two octaves above Middle C. It is less accurate than phase detection except at very high frequencies of 8000 hertz and above when the pinna (the part of the ear which protrudes from the head) becomes an effective aid as a focussing device. Animals with small heads cannot use phase differences for localizing sounds because the time intervals are too short. But they tend to be able to hear very high-pitched sounds, and are therefore able to make use of the sonic shadows which their heads form in the path of sound waves shorter than the diameter of their heads.

In 1940, Hans Wallach performed an experiment in which a continuous sound source was kept directly in front of the subject's nose by means of a special apparatus even when the subject turned his head from left to right. Because this head movement did not result in any phase or intensity differences between the signals reaching his ears, the subject reported that the sound source seemed to be directly overhead. His brain had performed a remarkable feat of logical deduction and come up with the wrong answer. Under normal circumstances, if the head is moved from left to right and the binaural pattern remains the same, it is logical to conclude that the sound source is either directly above or directly below, and experience teaches that in such cases it is nearly always above.

Wallach also devised the experiment with the rotating drum described in the question. In this case the subject is motionless, but a slight illusion of movement is created by the rotation of the drum. Since the sound source and the subject are in fact stationary, the pattern of binaural signals remains constant. Once again, the brain puts all this information together, performs some computations and logical deductions, and concludes that the sound source is directly overhead. The illusion is very powerful: it persists even if the subject is aware of the true situation.

References: Rosenzweig, M.R. Auditory localization. *Scientific American,* 1961, **205**(4), 132-7.
Wallach, H. The role of head movements and vestibular and visual cues in sound localization. *Journal of Experimental Psychology,* 1940, **27,** 339-68.

7 (k, l). Score one point for realizing that none of the tones would be distinguished from the first, and another for correctly identifying only 1018 watts and 1024 watts as distinguishable from 1000 watts. The first question should be correctly answered by anyone familiar with Weber's law; the second requires not only a familiarity with the law, but also a recollection of the appropriate Weber fraction.

In 1846, the German physiologist Ernst Heinrich Weber discovered a fundamental law in the area of sensation. It can be most easily explained in terms of a simple example. If a person can just barely detect the difference in weight between an object of 530 grams and one of 540 grams, then how heavy would an object have to be to be just barely distinguishable from one of 1060 grams? The answer is not 1070 grams but 1080 grams. According to the same principle, a weight of 265 grams will be just barely distinguishable from one of 270 grams. The general principle, which should be obvious from this example, is that the smallest increase which can be detected in the weight of an object is in direct proportion to the original weight; the heavier the original weight, the larger the increase which can just be detected. This is equivalent to saying that the 'just noticeable difference' between two weights is a constant fraction of the lighter weight. Numerous experiments have shown that this fraction is in fact 1/53.

Having established this law in the case of weight discrimination, Weber went on to show that the same general principle applies to sensations of the pitch of musical tones, the loudness of tones, the brightness of lights, and other sensory experiences. The simplicity of the law is surprising, but most people are dimly aware that some such principle is at work in various areas of experience. A journey of 20 miles, for example, seems much longer than one of 10 miles, but a journey of 120 miles would seem hardly any longer than one of 110 miles.

Weber's law is nowadays usually expressed in symbols. This amounts to nothing more than a more compact way of expressing the idea which Weber described in words and examples. The mathematical form of Weber's law is

$$\frac{\Delta I}{I} = k.$$

In this formula, ΔI represents the *just noticeable difference* in physical 'intensity' (weight of objects, frequency or amplitude of tones, brightness of lights, and so on); it is also called the *difference threshold* or *difference limen*. The Greek Letter Delta (Δ) stands for *difference,* and the Roman letter I stands for *intensity*. In the first example above, the difference threshold (ΔI) is equal to 10 grams. I represents the absolute physical intensity of the less intense stimulus; in the same example $I = 530$ grams. Finally, k is a constant called the *Weber fraction.* The Weber fraction is constant for any given type of sensory discrimination but differs from one type to the next. The Weber fraction for lifted weights, for example, is 1/53, as shown in the examples above. For pitch discrimination, $k = 1/333$; for loudness discrimination, $k = 1/11$; for visual brightness discrimination, $k = 1/62$; and so on. The important point to note is that in each case the just noticeable difference (ΔI), expressed as a fraction of the intensity of the lesser stimulus $(\Delta I/I)$, is a constant (k).

Weber's law holds remarkably accurately over most of the usable range of intensity for nearly all types of sensation. Like Boyle's law in physics, however, it breaks down at the extremes. For visual discriminations of various kinds, the law holds across 99.9 per cent of the range of intensities which can be used, namely those which can be sensed without damage to the eyes. For loudness discrimination, the Weber fraction remains obediently constant across no less than 999,999-millionths of the usable range. The audible range for pitch discrimination extends from about 20 hertz to about 20,000 hertz, but the Weber fraction is 1/333 only for tones above 500 hertz: it is larger for lower pitches.

Applying Weber's law to the first question, we note first of all that the difference threshold at 1000 hertz is given as 3 hertz. It follows that $3/1000 = k = 0.003$. This agrees, incidentally, with the Weber fraction of 1/333 for pitch discrimination established by experiments. At 2000 hertz we therefore have $\Delta I/2000 = 0.003$, which yields $\Delta I = 6$. In other words, a person would not be able to distinguish a tone of 2000 hertz from one of less than 2006 hertz. All of the values given fall below this critical level, so none would be distinguishable from the original.

It may seem surprising that these answers can be stated in a general way for all listeners. The answers are indeed valid for everyone, provided of course that there is no serious damage to the ears or auditory nerve structures. But a word needs to be said about the fact that some people have a better 'sense of pitch' than others, and some are described as being 'tone deaf'. The truth of the matter is that virtually anyone can be trained to recognize differences in pitch corresponding to the Weber fraction $k = 1/333$ under ideal listening conditions. 'Tone deafness' does not arise from an inability to *hear* differences in pitch; it is rather an inability to *recognize* or *interpret* what is heard. A 'tone deaf' listener does not know what to listen for. The handicap is analogous to dyslexia (word blindness): in both cases the problem usually arises from a failure to recognize or interpret what is perceived, rather than any failure of the process of perception itself.

Turning to the second question, it is interesting to note first of all that visual brightness discrimination is much less sensitive than auditory pitch discrimination. In fact auditory pitch discrimination is by far the most sensitive type of sensory ability a human being possesses. This is indicated by the relatively small Weber fraction for auditory pitch discrimination.

Even a competent psychologist would stumble on the second question unless the appropriate Weber fraction for visual brightness discrimination (1/62) could be retrieved from memory. Bearing this figure in mind, and applying Weber's law to the information given in the question, we find that $\Delta I/1000 = 1/62$, which yields $\Delta I = 16$. This is, of course, the just noticeable difference asked for in the question. A light of 1016 watts or more would therefore seem noticeably brighter than one of 1000 watts. Of the alternatives listed, only the last two fall within this range.

Reference: Stevens, S.S. Decibels of light and sound.
          Physics Today, 1955, **8** (10), 12-17.

8 (g, k). Score one point for realizing that seven further candles would have to be lit, another for concluding that Sauce B contained less than half a teaspoon of salt, and a third bonus point for correctly stating the power law (see below). Even a trained psychologist would be unlikely to get full marks on this question without remembering certain crucial figures obtained from experiments on the brightness of lights and the saltiness of tastes.

We are concerned here, as in Question 7, with the relationship between (psychological) sensations and the (physical) stimuli which cause them. This area of research is therefore known as *psychophysics*; it is the oldest branch of experimental psychology. The central problem of psychophysics is this: How is the intensity of sensation related to stimulus intensity? The relationship is not a straightforward one, as the following simple *Gedankenexperiment* (imaginary experiment) shows. Imagine entering a completely dark room, and switching on first one, then a second 100-watt lamp. The physical intensity of the illumination would be doubled when the second lamp was switched on, but the room would not seem twice as brightly lit as before; in fact, it would seem only very slightly brighter. At least in this case, the intensity of sensation is evidently not related to stimulus intensity in an obvious way.

The first person to understand this problem clearly was the German philosopher and mystic Gustav Theodor Fechner (1801-78). Fechner was one of the most bizarre geniuses in the history of psychology. Some of his earlier books are devoted to discussing the comparative anatomy of angels and proving that the moon is made of iodine. On the morning of October 22 1850, before rising from his bed, he came up with a more useful idea which struck him like a revelation. It was that equal increases in sensation correspond to equal *proportional* increases in stimulus intensity; or put another way, sensations increase by equal amounts

whenever the physical intensity of stimuli increase by equal percentages. For example, according to Fechner, the sensation of increase in brightness caused by a rise in light intensity from 60 watts to 180 watts is the same as that caused by a rise from 100 watts to 300 watts. This is because the number of watts (the intensity of the stimulus) increases by the same proportional amount or percentage in each case (it is trebled). As this example shows, Fechner's suggestion can be expressed in the following way: sensation increases by equal steps (an arithmetic series) while the stimulus increases by equal percentages (a geometric series).

Fechner thought that he had discoverd a fundamental law of great importance to one of the central problems of philosophy, namely the mind-body problem (see Chapter 5). He spent the following 10 years performing experiments to test the validity of the law for various types of sensation. From 1855 to 1859, for example, he made no fewer than 67,072 weight comparisons, using himself as both experimenter and subject. In 1860 his *Elements of Psychophysics* was published. In this work, he defined psychophysics as 'an exact science of the functional relation or relations of dependency between body and mind'.

How can Fechner's law be expressed in the simplest possible mathematical formula? The key lies in the fact that an arithmetic series is related to a geometric series as logarithms are related to their corresponding numbers. Everyone who has used tables of logarithms knows, for example, that the common logarithms 1, 2, 3, 4, ... , correspond to the numbers 10, 100, 1000, 10,000, ... ; the logarithms increase by equal steps in arithmetic series while the numbers increase by tenfold proportions in geometric series. Fechner therefore suggested that 'the increase of sensation and stimulus stand in a similar relation to that of the increase of a logarithm and a number'. Accordingly, if we represent the intensity of sensation by ψ (the Greek letter psi, short for *psy*chological) and stimulus intensity by ϕ (Greek phi, short for *phy*sical), Fechner's law can be expressed as follows:

$$\psi = k \log \phi .$$

In this formula, k is simply a constant which depends upon the type of sensation being considered. The units in which stimulus intensity is measured are those of barely detectable stimuli at the threshold of sensation.

For almost a century from the time of Fechner's *Elements*, psychologists believed that the logarithmic law was basically valid, although its predictions were not always found to be quite accurate by experimenters. A number of practical uses were found for it. Perhaps the best known practical application is the decibel scale of sound intensity. A decibel is one tenth of a bel (named after Alexander Graham Bell, the inventor of the telephone). Using Fechner's formula, with $k = 10$ and ϕ equal to sound intensity, usually expressed in units of a barely audible sound, ψ gives the decibel level. Since the logarithm of 2 is about 0.3, it follows that whenever the intensity of a sound is doubled, the decibel level rises by 3 units (10 x 0.3). On the decibel scale, conversational speech registers at about 60 dB; if two people speak at once, the phsyical sound intensity is doubled, but the decibel level rises to only 63 dB. The decibel scale is used by broadcasting and telephone engineers, and laws governing industrial and environmental noise are based upon it in many parts of the world.

Unfortunately, however, Fechner's law does not describe the sensation-stimulus relationship correctly. During the 1960s, largely as a result of the work of the American psychologist S. Smith Stevens, it became clear that a slightly different law gives much more accurate results. The modern power law, as it is usually called, makes predictions which have turned out to be astonishingly exact when tested by experiments. According to the power law, the relationship between sensation and stimulus intensity is not one of an arithmetic series to a geometric series as Fechner believed; it is rather a relationship of one geometric series and another. To put it another way, equal percentage increases in sensation correspond to equal percentage increases in stimulus intensity, but the two percentages are not necessarily equal. For example, the sensation of loudness is doubled whenever the intensity of a sound is multiplied by 2.8. The mathematical formula for the power law is

$$\psi = k \phi^n$$

where ψ is the intensity of sensation, k is a constant scale factor which depends upon the units of measurement, ϕ is the intensity of the stimulus, and n is an exponent which is fixed for any given type of sensation but varies from one type to the next.

The exponents for various types of sensation have been determined through experiments. For some types of sensation, such as visual brightness ($n = 0.33$), the exponents are small. In these cases a doubling of stimulus intensity produces a somewhat smaller percentage change in sensation, as shown in the *Gedankenexperiment* of going into a dark room and switching on lights. Under these conditions, Fechner's logarithmic law and the modern power law happen to give very similar results. But when large exponents apply, as in the sensation of electric shock, ($n = 3.5$) and saline (salty) taste ($n = 1.4$), a doubling of stimulus intensity produces an even greater percentage increase in sensation, and in such cases only the power law describes the sensation-stimulus relationship correctly. Fechner's law thus provides an excellent approximation to the more exact power law in some cases but not in others.

Turning now to the first part of the question, we note that the intensity of the stimulus is initially the light of one single candle. In this case, therefore, $\phi = 1$. The exponent for visual brightness has been found in numerous experiments to be 0.33, therefore $n = 0.33$. We may accordingly describe the initial situation as follows:

$$\psi = k(1)^{0.33}.$$

After a certain (unknown) number of further candles are lit, the sensation of brightness is doubled. In mathematical symbols,

$$2\psi = k(\phi)^{0.33}.$$

We need to solve these two equations simultaneously to find the value of ϕ. This is most easily done by dividing each side of the second equation by the corresponding sides of the first. Since the left- and right-hand sides of the first equation represent the same quantity — this follows from the fact that it is an equation — we can divide each side of the second equation by this quantity. Dividing 2ψ by ψ and $k(\phi)^{0.33}$ by $k(1)^{0.33}$ we get

$$2 = \frac{\phi^{0.33}}{1^{0.33}} .$$

Solving this equation for ϕ, we finally arrive at $\phi = 8$. This means that an illumination eight times as strong as that produced by a single candle would cause the sensation of brightness to be doubled. In other words, seven further candles would have to be lit.

In the second part of the question, Sauce A contained a quarter of a teaspoon of salt and Sauce B contained an unknown amount (ϕ). Sauce B tasted twice as salty as Sauce A. The psychologist referred to in the question had only to remember that the exponent for saline tasting is greater than 1 to realize that Sauce B must have contained less than twice as much salt as Sauce A. A more precise solution can be worked out by putting all the known facts including the appropriate exponent of $n = 1.4$ into two equations, one for each sauce:

$$\psi = k(\tfrac{1}{4})^{1.4} \quad \text{and}$$

$$2\psi = k(\phi)^{1.4} .$$

Once again, we can divide each side of the second equation by the corresponding side of the first. Thus

$$2 = \frac{\phi^{1.4}}{\left(\tfrac{1}{4}\right)^{1.4}} ,$$

which can be solved to give $\phi = 0.4$. Sauce B therefore contained four tenths of a teaspoon of salt.

Reference: Stevens, S.S. *Psychophysics and Social Scaling.*
Morristown, NJ: General Learning
Corporation, 1972.

9. (a). Score one point. The note sounds louder and — to most listeners — slightly lower in pitch. This auditory illusion was discovered a long time ago, but it is not widely known. Like many of the familiar visual illusions, it has not been fully explained by psychologists.

A vibration of the ear-drum, in order to be perceived as a sound, needs to be converted into nerve impulses and transmitted to the brain. The way this is achieved is rather complicated, but it has been clarified to a large extent by the work of the Hungarian researcher, Georg von Békésy, which earned him a Nobel prize in 1961.

When sound waves strike the ear-drum, they cause it to vibrate. The vibration is transmitted via three tiny bones in the middle ear, namely the hammer, anvil, and stirrup, to a coiled-up tube in the inner ear known as the *cochlea* (from the Greek word for snail). The cochlea is filled with fluid. The vibration of the stirrup causes waves to travel through this fluid along the length of the cochlea. Running down the middle of the cochlea is a flexible membrane called the *basilar membrane*. Since the fluid-filled chamber is broad at one end and narrow at the other, a wave travelling through it has the effect of causing a maximum vibration of the basilar membrane in a particular region depending upon the wave frequency. Resting on the basilar membrane is a structure covered with upright-standing *hair cells*. The auditory nerves are attached to this structure around the bases of the hair cells. When the basilar membrane vibrates, it bends the hair cells in the corresponding region back and forth. This excites a particular group of nerve fibres which transmit impulses to specific areas of the brain. The pitch of a note is determined by which part of the basilar membrane vibrates maximally and *which nerves* are therefore excited. The volume of a sound is determined by the strength of vibration of the basilar membrane and the amount of movement of the hair cells, which is translated into the *rate* at which the nerves fire. But the picture is complicated by the fact that, for very low-frequency sounds, the rate of neural firing apparently also acts as a method of coding pitch.

The sensitivity of the ear is almost beyond belief. The weakest sound signal which can be heard is one with an amplitude of about 1.25×10^{-10} centimetres. A sound wave of this amplitude moves the ear-drum back and forth across a distance equivalent to one four-millionth of the diameter of a fine silk fibre, or one tenth of the diameter of a hydrogen atom! The corresponding movement of the basilar membrane which transmits the signal to the auditory nerves is 100 times smaller. For most purposes, the ear manages to perform as an extremely high-fidelity sound system. But it is hardly surprising that in certain circumstances minor distortions creep in.

The distortion hinted at in the question was first noticed during the nineteenth century; it was confirmed in a series of rigorous experiments by Fletcher, Snow, and Stevens in the 1930s. This is a tendency for certain tones to sound lower in pitch when they are made louder, even though their objective frequencies are fixed. The experiments showed, however, that this effect is restricted to tones below about 2000 to 3500 hertz (the top octave of the piano). For higher tones, exactly the opposite distortion occurs: high-pitched tones sound even higher when they grow louder.

The Fletcher illusion, as it may be called, is experienced by most people at least to some extent. A few hear hardly any change in pitch with increased volume, while others hear a sharpening or flattening with very loud tones amounting to 35 per cent, a pitch change of about five semitones. The effect is strongest when pure tones such as those of amplified tuning forks are used. The Fletcher illusion has important implications for musical performance. Keyboard players cannot compensate for the distortion because the pitches of the notes are fixed, but string players, for example, ought to make the necessary corrections when playing loud passages. Experiments by Lewis and Cowan have shown that violinists and cellists do not in general make any corrections for the effect.

No convincing explanation has yet been suggested for the Fletcher illusion. It seems fairly safe to assume, however, that it is connected in some way with the delicacy of the auditory apparatus in the middle and inner ears. For reasons as yet unknown, this apparatus is apparently unable to transmit very strong mechanical vibrations from the ear-drum to the basilar membrane without distortion.

References: Békésy, G. von. *Experiments in Hearing*, translated and edited by E.G. Wever. New York: McGraw-Hill, 1960.

Seashore, C.E. *Psychology of Music.* New York: McGraw-Hill, 1938.

10 (b). Score one point. Richard is virtually certain to have judged the smaller can to be much heavier than the larger one. The illusion is powerful and reliable. In an experiment on 100 military officers, for example, the American psychologist Richard Crutchfield used two 300-gram objects, one of which was twice as wide and twice as deep as the other. The subjects were told that the larger object weighed 300 grams, and were invited to guess the weight of the smaller one. The average estimate was 750 grams; in other words, overestimates were in the region of two and a half times the correct weight. In some cases, the errors were as large as sevenfold.

The size-weight illusion, as it is called, is not quite as easy to explain as it seems. When people read abstract descriptions of it, they usually assume that it can be explained by the surprise which subjects experience when they lift the second can. If a person lifts the larger can first, for example, he then expects the smaller can to feel lighter; thus when he comes to lift the smaller can he is surprised by its heaviness. According to this theory, the smaller can feels heavier than it really is because it feels heavier than it is expected to feel in comparison with the larger can. The same explanation in reverse applies if the smaller can is lifted first; in this case the second can feels lighter than it really is because it is lighter than it is expected to be in comparison with the smaller can. An essential feature of this explanation is the unexpectedness or surprisingness of the weight of the second can.

Unfortunately, this simple explanation does not seem to fit the facts. Experiments have shown that the illusion persists even if the two cans are lifted over and over again. It is not even destroyed by a knowledge of the objective facts: the illusion remains even after a subject has been allowed to look inside the cans, or even to weigh them on a balance. In these cases the element of surprise is no longer present: the subject knows what to expect when he lifts the second can.

A different explanation which does not rely on unexpectedness or surprise is needed.

The alert reader may have noticed a certain resemblance between the size-weight illusion and the failure to master the conservation of mass in pre-operational children (see the answer to Question 4). The pre-operational child thinks that the weight of a lump of plasticine is changed when it is moulded into a different shape. The size-weight illusion can be explained by a different kind of conservation failure: adults are apparently unable to master the conservation of mass when volume rather than shape is altered. They think that the weight of an object is changed when its volume is changed.

If two tin cans weigh the same, but one is twice as wide and twice as deep as the other, then school physics shows that the larger can has eight times the volume of the smaller one. The smaller can is therefore eight times as dense as the larger one in grams per cubic centimetre. The adult who experiences the size-weight illusion centres on the differences in density between the two objects without sufficiently taking into account the differences in volume. The smaller of the two cans seems heavier because it is denser. The size-weight illusion is not, however, due to a failure to grasp the difference between mass and density at an intellectual level, since even professors of physics experience it.

Reference: Crutchfield, R.S., Woodworth, D.G., and Albrecht, R.E. *Perceptual Performance and the Effective Person.* San Antonio: Air Force Personnel and Training Research Center, 1955.

11 (d). Score one point for bravery. The image will indeed appear in full natural colour. This astonishing phenomenon was discovered accidentally by Edwin Land, the inventor of the polaroid camera, and reported in 1959. It refutes the fallacy that the colour of an object in the visual field is determined by the wavelength of the light reflected by it.

The fundamental properties of the rainbow were discovered by Isaac Newton in 1666. Later physicists discovered the wave properties of light and showed that the visible spectrum extends from wavelengths of about 400 millimicrons (millionths of a millimetre) at the 'violet' end to about 700 millimicrons at the 'red' end. In the nineteenth century, James Clerk Maxwell and Hermann von Helmholtz found that by mixing light from the red, green, and blue bands of the spectrum, all spectral colours could be created. On this basis they proposed a theory of colour vision in terms of the three 'primary' colours. The fundamental idea of this classical *component theory* was that the eye contains three kinds of mechanisms for responding to colour: red, green, and blue receptors which respond only to long, medium, and short waves respectively. According to this theory, all colour sensations result from the degrees to which the three receptors are stimulated. It was widely believed from that time on that the colour seen at any point in the field of vision could be fully explained by the wavelength or wavelengths coming from that point.

Land's experiment demonstrates that this common belief is untenable. The light reflected by the screen is composed entirely of 'red' and 'white' light. According to classical notions, the mixture of red and white can produce nothing but pink. If we remove the black-and-white slides from the projectors, the screen does indeed look pink, but as soon as we slot them back into position the full colour effect is instantly re-created: the apples look green, the plums look blue, and the bananas look yellow; even non-spectral colours (those which are not found in the rainbow) like browns can be clearly seen. Yet the slides are capable only of permitting more or less 'red' or 'white' light to pass through at various points.

Colour vision is more subtle than is commonly realized. There is no such thing, strictly speaking, as 'red', 'white' or 'green' light. The colours seen in a natural image are determined not by their absolute wavelengths, but by the relative balance of long and short wavelengths across the entire visual field. Component theories of colour vision have been supported, but have also had to be radically revised, following the recent discovery of primary colour pigments in the eyes of various animals. Each of the cells associated with these pigments has been shown to be maximally sensitive to either short, medium, or long-wave light, but each responds to a lesser degree to wavelengths extending across most of the visible spectrum. When the wavelengths present in the visual field are artificially biased towards one part of the spectrum, as in Land's experiment, the eye-brain computer makes an instantaneous adjustment. The various levels of response of the primary colour receptors are interpreted in terms of this fact in a manner which restores the natural balance of perceived colour. A wavelength of, for example, 550 millimicrons has no inherent colour in itself: it may be seen as red or green or blue or brown depending on the range of wavelengths present in the entire field of vision.

References: Land, E.H. Experiments in color vision. *Scientific American*, 1959, **200**(5), 84-9.
Land, E.H. The retinex theory of color vision. *Scientific American*, 1977, **237**(6), 108-28.

12 (a, c). Score one point for realizing that Leon's attitude is likely to have become less favourable towards the pay demand, and a bonus point for predicting that his attitude is likely to have changed more if he was paid a small amount. This apparently surprising relationship between incentive and attitude change has been found in scores of experiments in the area of *cognitive dissonance.*

The theory of cognitive dissonance, proposed by the American psychologist Leon Festinger in 1957, deals with the way in which people handle items of knowledge which are psychologically inconsistent. Two items of knowledge, or *cognitions,* are considered dissonant if one creates an expectation of the converse of the other. The cognition A: *I smoke cigarettes* is, for example, dissonant with B: *Cigarette smoking damages my health,* provided that I wish to be in good health. Dissonance has motivating effects: it creates a drive to reduce the dissonance in the way thirst creates a drive to drink or hunger a drive to eat. In the case of dissonance, the drive can be eliminated only by reversing one of the cognitions. In the cigarette-smoking illustration, for example, the dissonance would be eliminated if I gave up smoking or persuaded myself that I had given it up although I had not done so, or if I completely rejected the evidence that smoking cigarettes damages my health. These methods of dissonance elimination may, however, be difficult or impossible to achieve. The dissonance can then be reduced to an extent by adding further cognitions which serve to justify the inconsistency, such as C1: *But I smoke only low-tar brands*; C2: *But I'm more likely to die in a road accident than from the effects of smoking*; C3: *But there will soon be a cure for lung cancer*; C4: *But I'd rather live a short, happy life than a long, deprived one*; and so on. The availability of cognitions which serve to justify the dissonance depends on circumstances.

Cognitive dissonance theory has been successfully applied to a wide range of psychological problems, from the behaviour of end-of-the-world cultists to the effects of making decisions, resisting temptation, and lying. In many cases, application of the theory has led to counter-intuitive predictions which have nevertheless been confirmed by experimental research.

Applying dissonance theory to the situation described in the question, we note that the dissonant cognitions are A: *I think the pay demand is reasonable,* and B: *I argued publicly that it is unreasonable.* Cognition B is effectively fixed, but cognition A is free to change if Leon alters his attitude towards the pay demand. Another important cognition which may provide a source of justification must also be taken into account: C: *But I was paid a large/small amount of money for giving the speech.* Its effectiveness as a justification depends on the size of the payment: if the amount was small, the justification is correspondingly weak and the drive to change Cognition A remains strong. If, on the other hand, the payment and thus the justification was large, the drive to change Cognition A is considerably reduced. Numerous experiments have confirmed the prediction of dissonance theory that a person's attitude changes in the direction of the point of view he argues, but only when the justification for doing so is small.

Reference: Festinger, L. *A Theory of Cognitive Dissonance.* Evanston, Ill.: Row, Peterson, 1957.

13 (c, f). Score one point for realizing that most people would have remembered approximately the same number of items, and another for deciding that with easier items, approximately the same number would have been remembered on average. These findings, which have been firmly established in the classical tradition of memory research, contradict widespread misconceptions about what it means to have a 'good memory' and about the connection between ease of learning and ease of remembering.

The systematic study of memory was pioneered by the German researcher, Hermann Ebbinghaus, in the 1880s. Ebbinghaus began experimenting with fragments of poetry, but found that they aroused all sorts of mental associations which affected the ease or difficulty of committing them to memory. He cast about for some kind of material which was relatively homogeneous, evoked few or no mental

associations, and was easily broken into objectively equal units suitable for quantitative investigation. Eventually he hit upon the idea of the nonsense syllable. Some thousands of nonsense syllables can easily be formed from consonant-vowel-consonant combinations, or CVC trigrams as they are often called today. With teutonic thoroughness, Ebbinghaus pursued his investigations by committing a number of lists of nonsense syllables to memory every week throughout a significant portion of his later life. More recent research has made use of both nonsense syllables and more meaningful material.

Three main factors have been found to affect the ease and speed of learning. The first is the subject's learning ability: some people learn material of all kinds much more quickly and easily than others. The second is the meaningfulness of the material: lists of simple words are much easier to learn than lists of nonsense syllables. The third is inter-item similarity: a list of very similar words or nonsense syllables tends to cause confusion and is harder to learn than a list of sharply distinctive items.

Turning now to the forgetting phase, two unexpected findings merit special attention. First, material which is difficult to learn is remembered equally as well as material which is easy to learn, provided that both types of material have been equally well learned in the first place. Given equal time for study, the difficult material will of course be retained less well. But experiments have shown this to be due entirely to the fact that it has been less well learned. What is important is the degree of learning; lists of words, names, nonsense syllables, telephone numbers, or chemical formulae which are learned to the same criterion display the same rate of forgetting.

Secondly, slow learners do not forget any more rapidly than quick learners. By definition, they require more time to learn material to a specified criterion, but having reached this level, all people of similar ages forget at approximately the same rate. In each of the experiments described in the question, for example, young adults would forget roughly 20 per cent of the items (four items) in 24 hours; older subjects would forget slightly more. This applies to material learned just sufficiently to produce one perfect immediate recall. Continuing learning beyond this point, if pursued diligently enough, can reduce this rate to near zero. Learning several sets of similar material increases the standard rate of forgetting through interference of earlier items with later ones (*proactive interference*) and of later items with earlier ones (*retroactive interference*). Many psychologists believe that all forgetting is due to proactive and retroactive interference of some kind. This may account partly for the decline of memory with age, since older people carry more potentially interfering material in their memory stores.

Reference: Underwood, B.J. *Experimental Psychology,* 2nd ed. New York: Meredith, 1966.

14 (b). Score one point. The second rat would display the habit for longer than the first rat. This finding has been replicated hundreds of times in *operant conditioning* experiments concerned with *reinforcement schedules*.

Operant conditioning is a method of investigating aspects of animal and human learning pioneered in the 1930s by the American psychologist, Burrhus F. Skinner. It is a more versatile alternative to the method of classical conditioning of the Nobel prizewinning Russian physiologist, Ivan P. Pavlov. In the jargon of modern operant theory, the rats referred to in the question were conditioned in *Skinner boxes.* The lever-pressing operant behaviour was strengthened by means of *positive reinforcement* in the form of food pellets. A *continuous* schedule of reinforcement was used with the first rat, and a *partial* reinforcement schedule was used with the second. When reinforcement is discontinued, the *operant level* or strength of the lever-pressing behaviour may be determined by counting the number of responses made until *extinction* of the behaviour is observed.

The techniques of operant conditioning have been applied to various types of behaviour in rats, pigeons, humans, and a wide range of other animals. Its effects are now well understood; the results are highly predictable and show surprisingly little variation from one species to the next. The operant technique known as *shaping* enables animals to be trained to behave in strange ways. This involves selectively reinforcing behaviour which resembles the desired response pattern more and more closely. In one famous application of shaping, for example, a number of pigs were trained to turn on a radio, eat at a table, run a vacuum cleaner over the floor, and put a pile of washing in a basket. In ordinary conversations, humans can be conditioned to increase the frequency with which they give opinions, talk about themselves and so forth, by being reinforced with smiles and other signs of approval. Shaping techniques have been widely used to modify problem behaviour in children and mental patients. Some 'behaviourist' psychologists, including Skinner, believe that all behaviour, virtually without exception, can be explained by operant conditioning which occurs in the natural environment. This view has increasingly been challenged following the work of Noam Chomsky and other experts on language, which has shown that conditioning cannot explain the facts of verbal behaviour.

Continuous and partial reinforcement schedules generate strikingly different patterns of behaviour, and different types of partial schedules have different effects. Partial schedules may be based upon the number of responses or the length of time elapsing between reinforcements. Each type of schedule produces a pattern of response which is almost identical whether it is observed in rats, pigeons or humans.

The experiments described in the question involved continuous and partial schedules. Compared to the former, the latter generate responses of remarkably high operant levels: an animal will typically expend much more energy than it gets in return in food reinforcements. A human equivalent is gambling: many people show high operant levels of behaviour which guarantee an expected net loss when confronted with partial reinforcement gambling machines such as one-armed bandits or fruit machines. Perhaps the most striking feature of partial reinforcement schedules is that they generate conditioned responses which are extremely resistant to extinction when the reinforcement is withdrawn. This well-established finding provides an answer to the question.

Reference: Skinner, B.F. *About Behaviorism.* New York: Alfred A. Knopf, 1974.

15 (b). Score one point. Exceptionally intelligent people are in general physically and mentally healthier than others. The evidence for this comes from various sources, by far the most detailed of which is the continuing study of 1528 exceptionally intelligent people initiated by Lewis Terman in the United States in the 1920s.

Terman's gifted sample, the 'termites' as they called themselves, were chosen from the Californian public school system in 1921. All had IQs above 135, which puts them in the top 1 per cent of the population in terms of IQ. Their ages at the beginning of the study ranged from three to 19 years. The sample turned out to be unrepresentative of the general population in various ways apart from intelligence. For example, 10.5 per cent of the 'termites' — and 17 per cent of those who were later most successful in their careers — were Jewish, compared with an estimated 5 per cent of Jews in the population from which they were selected. Approximately one third came from professional families, although only 3 per cent of the general population fell into this category in 1921.

The 'termites' were tested and interviewed in 1922, 1928, 1940, 1950, 1955, 1960, and 1972. Some died and others vanished along the way, but three quarters of the original sample were still available for the 1972 follow-up, and the sample is not expected to become extinct until the year 2010. The results of the first 35 years of the investigation are contained in the five volumes of Terman's *Genetic Studies of Genius.* Subsequent reports have appeared at irregular intervals since then. After Terman's death in 1956, the project was carried on by others. Among the younger psychologists who took over the directorship of the project was Robert Sears, a professor of psychology who later revealed that he was himself a member of the original sample of 'termites'.

As children, the 'termites' were found to be generally above average on a wide range of measures of physical and mental health. A high proportion, though not as many as some might have expected, have been outstandingly successful in their careers. Their occupations range from sandwich-shop attendant and postman to brigadier-general and university professor. Their average income in adult life has been about four times the national average. The female 'termites' were ahead of their time in adopting life-styles which later became fashionable on a wider scale. They tended to marry later, have fewer children and have them later in life, and remain single more often than others of their generation. A large proportion of them went out to work, and they turned out to be much happier in their work than other working women, possibly because they tended to get better jobs. The physical and mental health of the surviving 'termites', both male and female, has remained generally 'good' to 'very good' compared with the rest of the population.

References: Terman, L.M. (ed.) *Genetic Studies of Genius,* Vols I-V. Stanford: Stanford University Press, 1925-59.
Goleman, D. 1528 little geniuses and how they grew. *Psychology Today,* 1980, **13**(9), 28-53.

16 (a). Score one point for supposing that schizophrenia is more common among unskilled working-class people than among the upper-middle class, and a bonus point for stating the reverse relationship between social class and childhood autism.

The disproportionately high rates of schizophrenia found in the lowest social classes in Western industrial societies is not fully understood. It has been argued that the class differences may be due to a bias of diagnosis: psychiatrists and clinical psychologists may be more hesitant about attaching the label of schizophrenia to patients of high socioeconomic status. This explanation has, however, been largely refuted by census studies in which initial diagnoses have been carefully checked for class biases. It is also inconsistent with the fact that some equally stigmatized disorders, such as childhood autism, are much more common in upper-middle class families, while others, like manic-depressive psychosis, show no consistent class differences.

A different kind of explanation is based upon the supposed *stresses* of an unspecified kind which are alleged to be more common or more severe in lower-class child-rearing practices or general life circumstances, but no specific social factors of this kind have been successfully identified. Explanations in terms of *social drift* are based on the assumption that schizophrenics are unable to hold down middle-class jobs and that they therefore tend to drift downwards in the social class system and accumulate at the lowest levels. The main weakness of this explanation is that while it can account for the greater prevalence (proportion of existing cases) of schizophrenia at the lowest class levels, it cannot satisfactorily explain the greater incidence (proportion of new occurrences) among people who originate from these levels. Research has, in any case, often failed to find evidence that schizophrenics have drifted downwards in social class. A refined version of this explanation, in terms of *social residue* effects, has therefore been put forward. According to this view, schizophrenics may not display downward drift so much as failure to rise in the class hierarchy to the same extent as non-schizophrenics. This would also tend to lead to a high rate in the lowest class levels.

All the suggested explanations for the class distribution of schizophrenia are conjectural. In the case of childhood autism and other disorders showing an upward class bias, the explanation has proved even more elusive. The facts are nevertheless no longer in dispute.

Reference: Hollingshead, A.B. and Redlich, F.C. *Social Class and Mental Illness: A Community Study.* New York: Wiley, 1958.

17 (a). Score one point. The disorder characterized by multiple personality falls into the category of neurosis. It is quite unrelated to schizophrenia and manic-depression, both of which are classified as psychotic rather than neurotic disorders (see Chapter 3).

The popular confusion of multiple personality with schizophrenia probably has something to do with the derivation of the word. The word *schizophrenia* was coined by the German physician Eugen Bleuler in 1911. It is derived from the Greek words *schizin* (to split) and *phren* (mind), and denotes a type of mental disorder characeized by a lack of connection between thought processes, emotions, and behaviour, or a splitting up of psychological functions. The splitting implied by the word is not intended to refer to the alternation between different personality types which is characteristic of the disorder of multiple personality.

Multiple personality is an extremely rare condition; only a few hundred cases have ever been reported. It is traditionally classified as a neurosis, or more particularly a dissociative form of hysteria. It is allied to fuge states, or periods of loss of memory during which an individual wanders from home, and to the slightly more common conversion forms of hysteria in which physical symptoms like paralyses, blindness, and deafness are found without any underlying organic disorder.

Reference: Mayer-Gross, W., Slater, E. and Roth, M.
Clinical Psychiatry, 3rd ed. London: Baltimore, 1969.

18 (b). Score one point. The group decisions are likely to have been more risky than the average of the individual decisions. This is an example of the *group polarization phenomenon.*

A special case of group polarization, known as the *risky shift,* was first discovered by the American psychologist Edward Ziller in the late 1950s. Since then, scores of investigators have confirmed that group decisions tend usually to be riskier than individual decisions. During the 1970s it was discovered that the process underlying the risky shift is a more general tendency for group decisions to amplify the dominant attitudes in the group. In the case of decisions involving risk, the dominant group attitude is usually (though not always) in a generally risky rather than a cautious direction. The tendency for mass meetings to result in more risky decisions than secret ballots in labour disputes, and the emergence of extremist trends in various social and political contexts, are often explicable in terms of group polarization.

Several explanations for this phenomenon have been suggested. The most satisfactory of these rests upon the idea of *social comparison*. In the case of risk, for example, this explanation is based on the assumption that people in our culture tend on the whole to admire risk rather than caution, and consequently like to consider themselves at least as willing as others to take risks. As a result of the cultural value associated with risk, people tend to overestimate their own propensity for risk-taking relative to others; during the course of a group discussion, however, most people discover that their own initial risk levels are not as high as those of some others, and they therefore shift in favour of greater risk in order to restore their self-images as people at least as willing as others to take chances. Each of the assumptions built into this explanation has been supported by experimental findings, and it is favoured above alternative explanations because it can be applied, with appropriate modifications, to all types of group polarization. Alternative explanations have, in any event, not withstood experimental tests satisfactorily, although they seem very plausible on the surface.

Reference: Myers, D.G. and Lamm, H. The group polarization phenomenon. *Psychological Bulletin*, 1976, **83**, 602-27.

19 (a). Score one point for identifying prohibition of sex between certain close relatives as the only one of the listed alternatives which is characteristic of all known human societies.

The rules governing sex and marriage differ dramatically from one society to the next. In Tibet, it is quite common for several brothers to share the same wife. Among the Sotho tribesmen of South Africa and in many other non-European societies, a positive obligation exists to marry a cross-cousin (a child of one's mother's brother or father's sister) wherever possible. The Pondo people of the Transkei have a strict set of taboos governing name avoidance by married women: a bride is forbidden to utter the names of her husband's elder brothers, her father-in-law and his brothers, or her husband's paternal grandfather, whether they are living or dead; she is not even allowed in ordinary conversation to use words which rhyme with any of these names. In spite of striking differences in sex and marriage customs, however, all these societies and all others which have been investigated, share one type of rule in common: they all prohibit sex and marriage between certain members (usually between all members) of the primary family unit. Cross-cultural differences in sexual attitudes and behaviour have been investigated not only by psychologists, but also by sociologists and social anthropologists, who share a common interest in this area.

Numerous explanations for the incest taboo have been offered. Sociologists have suggested that the taboo serves the function of maintaining important networks of social relationships without which societies would break down into nuclear family units and disintegrate. Societies without any incest taboos are thus claimed to have been eliminated by natural selection. This functional explanation rests on the dubious assumption that if it were not for the taboo, everyone would naturally desire to mate with and marry close relatives. It also fails to explain why there is a taboo on sexual intercourse rather than simply a taboo on marriage with close relatives. A second type of explanation rests on genetic assumptions. According to this view, inbreeding would in the long run lead to the genetic deterioration and ultimate extinction of any society which practised it, so the incest taboo is alleged to have evolved by a similar kind of natural selection to that proposed by the functionalists. This explanation leaves open the question of why lower animals have not evolved similar incest taboos, and it is weakened by the existence in many societies of positive obligations to marry certain blood relatives, such as the cross-cousin rules mentioned earlier. Both functional and genetic theories lack a psychological dimension: even if we grant the dire sociological or biological consequences of incest, the problem remains of explaining why individual members of any society avoid practising it. The most satisfactory psychological explanation asserts that intimate contact between people before puberty, such as occurs in the primary family unit, leads to a lack of sexual attraction between them in later life. This theory is strongly supported by evidence from Israeli kibbutzim: these communal farms are organized in such a way that contact between unrelated children reared on the same kibbutz is intimate, and marriages virtually always take place between members of different kibbutzim in spite of pressure from parents to marry within the kibbutz.

Turning now to the second part of the question, it is necessary to say something about the work of the eminent Polish social anthropologist, Bronislaw Malinowski. During the First World War, Malinowski discovered a society in North-Western Melanesia in which the knowledge of the connection between sexual intercourse and pregnancy was unquestionably lacking. More recent investigations have revealed that these people, the Trobriand Islanders, continue to this day dogmatically denying any such connection in spite of numerous attempts by missionaries and others to explain the facts of life to them. Pig farming, which is a vital part of Trobriand food production, is severely hampered by this dogma, since even sows are thought to fall pregnant through causes unconnected with sexual intercourse.

According to the Trobriand Islanders, a woman conceives as a result of one of the spirits of her dead relatives being placed on her forehead while she sleeps. Blood from her body rushes to her head and carries the spirit-child to her womb. The blood continues to nourish the foetus after conception, which is why menstruation ceases when she falls pregnant. The suggestion that sexual intercourse causes pregnancy is treated by the Trobriand Islanders as ignorant and absurd. Facial resemblances between father and child are explained by a supposed imprinting of the father's features on those of the unborn spirit-child during intimate contact with the mother while she is pregnant. All sorts of arguments and evidence are produced to refute the sexual intercourse theory. Malinowski, for example, was told of a blind and feeble-minded Trobriand woman with a hideous face and a deformed body who was so overwhelmingly unattractive that no man, it seemed, could possibly have wanted to have sexual intercourse with her. Yet she had had a child, as the natives triumphantly pointed out whenever he raised the topic of sexual intercourse and pregnancy. Another popular argument is that many women who are sexually promiscuous (and there are few Trobriand virgins beyond eight years old) never have children. One informant told Malinowski how, after an absence of two years, he returned home and was delighted to find his wife with a new-born baby. He volunteered this information as final proof that sexual intercourse can have nothing to do with pregnancy.

The evidence regarding homosexuality can be dealt with quite briefly. Many societies have been found in which homosexuality is tolerated, approved of, or even obligatory. Among the Keraki of New Guinea and the Aranda of Australia, for example, male adolescents after initiation are required to take a passive role in anal intercourse for a full year; this is followed by a long period of active homosexuality until they are ready for heterosexual marriage. Approximately 64 per cent of societies for which evidence is available consider homosexuality acceptable for at least some people at some times. A few, such as the Etero and Marind-anim of New Guinea, are primarily homosexual, but these societies have some difficulty in maintaining their population numbers!

References: Ford, C.S. and Beach, F.A. *Patterns of Sexual Behavior.* New York: Harper, 1951.
Fox, R. *Kinship and Marriage.*
Harmondsworth: Penguin, 1967.
Malinowski, B. *The Sexual Life of Savages in North-Western Melanesia,* 3rd ed. London: Routledge and Kegan Paul, 1932.

20 (a, b, c). Score one point for realizing that a majority of
the committee members may have preferred Brown to
Carter, Brown to Adams, and Carter to Adams. The fact
that simple majority voting can produce a winner even
though a majority of the voters prefers each of the losing
alternatives to this winner is a paradox known as the *Borda
effect*. It is not a well-known voting paradox, but the
question could have been answered correctly by logical
deduction without any specialized knowledge of the Borda
effect.

The French mathematician and navigator, Jean-Charles
de Borda, first drew attention to the paradox shortly before
the outbreak of the French Revolution. It is most easily
explained in terms of a specific example. Suppose that the
seven committee members were each requested to place the
three candidates in order of preference. One possible
outcome is shown below.

| | *Committee members* | | | | | | |
	1	2	3	4	5	6	7
Most preferred alternative	A	A	A	B	B	C	C
Second most preferred alternative	B	B	B	C	C	B	B
Least preferred alternative	C	C	C	A	A	A	A

In this case, committee members 4, 5, 6 and 7 all prefer
Brown to Adams. They also all prefer Carter to Adams. The
paradox emerges if we ask what would happen if these seven
committee members were to choose one of the candidates by
means of a simple majority vote. Each would presumably
vote for the alternative he or she most preferred (unless
strategic voting was used, in which case other paradoxes
might emerge). Thus three committee members (1, 2 and 3)
would vote for Adams, two (4 and 5) would vote for Brown,
and two (6 and 7) would vote for Carter. This means that
Adams would get a majority of the votes (and he would
therefore be appointed to the vacant post) in spite of the fact
that a majority of the committee members prefers each of the
other candidates to Adams. In a very real sense, Adams is the

least preferred candidate: a majority of the committee members considers him the worst alternative of the three.

In committees choosing among three alternatives, the Borda effect cannot occur when there are less than seven voting members. In seven-member committees it can occur as shown in the example. It cannot occur in eight-member committees, oddly enough, but in committees or electorates larger than eight the effect is always a possibility. How often it occurs in practice is a matter to be settled by empirical research. It has been shown that the likelihood of the effect increases with the size of the voting group and is quite high with very large electorates. There is evidence to show that it has happened in at least one British general election; it is known to have occurred, for instance, in 1966.

Reference: Colman, A.M. and Pountney, I. The likelihood of the Borda effect in a British general election. *Behavioral Science,* 1978, **23**, 15-20.

Interpretation of Scores

Now add up your points. Check that you have awarded yourself points for completely correct answers only. In awarding bonus points you must use your own judgment of whether your answers were correct or not.

If you have worked through the quiz carefully and studied the explanations, you should have gained some intuitive notion of the nature and scope of psychology. If you used to believe that psychology is nothing but common sense, the experience should have proved particularly enlightening. In any event, you will no doubt have learned something about human behaviour.

The questions do not represent an entirely balanced selection from a typical undergraduate syllabus in psychology. The choice of topics was constrained in a number of ways. In the first place, the questions were specifically chosen to trip you up; they were based on ideas and research findings which are on the whole unexpected or about which there is widespread misunderstanding. They also had to be chosen from among topics which lend themselves to straightforward question-and-answer presentation, and questions which would have needed detailed background information in order to be understood had to be excluded. Only well-established findings were considered for inclusion; for this reason many of the problems are no longer considered to be live issues in psychology. Finally, the author's personal interests have inevitably played a part in biasing the selection. But, bearing all these qualifications in mind, the quiz does not give too misleading an idea of the subject matter of psychology. At least two thirds of the questions deal with topics which are considered basic knowledge in most degree courses. Nevertheless, not all these questions could be answered easily by psychology graduates. The questions on psychophysics (Questions 7 and 8) are, for example, very difficult: psychophysics is dealt with in all reputable degree courses, but many students never attain enough familiarity with it to solve problems like these.

The maximum possible score on the quiz is 30. Had the quiz been sprung on the author, he would probably have scored about 25 points. An interpretation of scores (which should not be taken too seriously!) is given below.

Score   *Interpretation*

  0-7   You were guessing; you have little specialized knowledge of psychology. But, since you completed the quiz, you probably have enough staying power to become an expert if you put your mind to it.

  8-12   Either you were guessing rather intelligently, or you have some specialized knowledge of psychology, or both.

13-17   You have read and understood a wide range of psychological literature.

18-22 You have reached the level of a good
psychology graduate.

23-27 You are a competent psychologist.

28-30 You are a cheat!

3. Aims and Methods of Psychology

Basic Research and Applied Psychology

The nature of psychology has been discussed in an abstract way in Chapter 1 and illustrated with examples in Chapter 2. Its fundamental aim can can be stated quite simply: it is to understand mental experience and behaviour. The examples given in Chapter 2 show how problems arise in explaining mental and behavioural phenomena, and how empirical research can sometimes help to solve these problems. Like any other branch of science, psychology aims to enlarge our understanding of the world; what distinguishes it from other scientific disciplines is the class of problems with which it deals. Basic research psychologists, like basic researchers in other fields, regard understanding and explanation as ends in themselves. A research contribution is considered important if it throws new light on a psychological phenomenon which was not properly understood before the research was carried out; it is not measured according to its immediate or potential 'usefulness' for solving practical (as opposed to theoretical) problems. The same is true, of course, of basic research in archaeology, quantum physics, astronomy, or any other scientific discipline.

The various fields of applied psychology, on the other hand, have practical aims in addition to the understanding or explaining of psychological phenomena. They are concerned with applications of psychological research findings to problems of everyday life. Applied psychology rests partly on the findings of basic research and partly on those of investigations specifically designed to answer practical questions. In clinical psychology, research on the nature, assessment, and treatment of mental disorders is applied in an effort to help disturbed people; in educational psychology, practical applications are found for research on learning and adjustment in school; and in industrial psychology, the conclusions of basic and applied research are addressed to problems of well-being and efficiency among people in work. In each of these fields of applied psychology the aims are largely practical: they focus on everyday problems. A more detailed discussion of applied psychology will be found in Chapter 6, which is devoted to psychology as a profession. The present chapter is concerned mainly with basic research, which forms the core of all first degree curricula in psychology. What follows is a brief outline of the major areas of basic psychological research, and a discussion of the most important methods used.

Areas of Psychological Research

Psychological research can be classified in a number of different ways. Early textbooks often divided psychology up into schools — structuralist, functionalist, behaviourist, and so on — but this method of classification lost most of its relevance after the decline of the schools in the 1930s and 1940s (see Chapter 5). Various systems of classification focus on the classes of organisms under investigation: thus it is possible to distinguish between child psychology on the one hand and adult psychology on the other, or between human and animal psychology, or between normal and abnormal psychology. Some classifications distinguish between experimental and 'correlational' psychology.

The method of classification which has become most popular in recent years is based upon the different categories of psychological *phenomena* which are investigated. The list of topic areas which serve as the chapter headings in most modern textbooks, and the course units in most undergraduate curricula are formed in this way. Classifications of this kind are not entirely satisfactory. In the first place, psychological research topics refuse to fall obligingly into watertight compartments; a certain amount of leakage between topic areas is inevitable, and some areas of investigation cannot be squeezed into single categories. There is a more serious problem associated with this method of classification. If it is strictly adhered to, it fails to do justice to the largely independent status of developmental, physiological, and social psychology. These areas of research are not defined in terms of (or, in the case of social psychology, not confined to) particular categories of psychological phenomena; they are concerned with certain *aspects* of *all* psychological phenomena. This difficulty is usually ignored — a fairly sensible way of dealing with it — and developmental, physiological, and social psychology are treated as though they had the same kind of logical status as any other. The 10 areas of research outlined below are the ones most often listed in textbooks and undergraduate curricula. The numbers in brackets after each sub-heading refer to the questions and explanations in Chapter 2 which fall wholly or partly into the research areas listed. The specific examples which are mentioned are intended to be indicative rather than exhaustive; it would be futile to try to list all of the topics investigated in contemporary psychological research.

1. States of consciousness (Chapter 2, Questions 1 and 2). Human beings exist in states of consciousness ranging from deep comas to episodes of heightened awareness often called 'peak' experiences. Research in this area in concerned with understanding these various types of consciousness. Since the mid-1950s, a vast amount of research has centred on sleep and dreams, and our understanding of these phenomena has been considerably enlarged. The phenomena associated with hypnosis have also been extensively investigated, although psychologists disagree about whether or not hypnosis can be regarded as a special state of consciousness. Research is also devoted to the effects of sensory deprivation, in which stimulation from sound, light, and touch is greatly diminished; conditions of this kind disturb perception, thinking, concentration, and intellectual functioning, and sometimes cause hallucinations similar to those experienced by schizophrenics. The effects of marihuana, LSD, and other drugs which alter the quality of consciousness are also investigated in this area.

2. Sensation and perception (3, 5, 6, 7, 8, 9, 10, 11). This is by far the oldest area of psychological research (see Chapter 5), and it is one in which impressive advances have been made. The bulk of research in this area is devoted to answering questions about how we see and hear, although other types of sensation and perception are also investigated. Colour vision is a particularly active research topic, which uncovers new problems as fast as it solves old ones. Psychophysical research on the relation between the intensity of light, sound, and other types of stimuli on the one hand, and the magnitude of sensation on the other, has continued throughout the history of experimental psychology. Auditory pitch perception and sound localization are quite well understood, although a number of puzzles remain. Numerous visual, auditory, and tactile illusions have been discovered, and researchers spend much time trying to understand them. A small but steady stream of research in this area is concerned with extra-sensory perception or ESP (see Chapter 1).

3. Learning, memory, and attention (5, 13, 14). In everyday usage, the word 'learning' often refers to the acquisition of knowledge; but the psychology of learning is concerned solely with the development of behaviour patterns or habits. A great deal of research, much of it based on experiments with rats, pigeons, and other non-human organisms, is devoted to this kind of learning. One branch of research on learning, for example, is concerned with the complicated manner in which rewards and punishments operate in the development of behaviour patterns. Research on memory investigates the ways in which people acquire knowledge; factors influencing the encoding, storage, and retrieval of information are studied, and attempts are made to provide explanations for forgetting. The remarkable and puzzling ability which humans and other animals have to pay attention only to certain important elements of the vast confusion of stimuli which bombard their sense organs is examined by research on attention. In general, we only attend to information which is potentially useful; but non-useful information must be processed at some level in the system in order to be excluded from attention, and much research in recent years has centred on the way in which we filter information to leave only what we require.

4. Language and thought (4, 10). Before the mid-1950s, most psychologists regarded speech as a form of skilled behaviour like any other, and relatively little research was devoted specifically to it. But following the work of Noam Chomsky (b. 1928) and others, it came to be recognized that, unlike other skills, speech is an essentially creative activity based upon an extremely complex and subtle system of largely unconscious rules, and psycholinguistics developed into an active area of research. Current ideas and research on language and thought have been strongly influenced by the development of electronic computers since the late 1940s, which has led to a new conception of the mind as an information-processing device. Research in this area centres on such matters as the way children acquire language, communication systems in animals, the nature and causes of speech errors, human problem-solving, the role of visual imagery in thinking, decision-making, creative thinking, and machine intelligence.

5. Motivation and emotion (12). Research on motivation is concerned with the reasons why people make choices or work towards certain goals rather than others, the factors which determine whether or not such goal-directed activity persists, and the degree of vigour or arousal which characterizes people's behaviour. Automatic, instinctive behaviour is common in animals low on the evolutionary scale, such as insects, but comparatively rare in humans. The behaviour of 'lower' animals can be explained to a large extent in terms of the biological needs of survival and reproduction, and does not usually exceed what these needs demand. Human beings, on the other hand, continue to pursue goal-directed activities after their biological needs are satisfied; human desires are virtually unlimited. Feelings

such as fear, anger, happiness, and sadness are investigated in research on emotion. Most psychologists would probably agree that research in this area, although it is concerned with important problems, has not produced very many impressive results.

6. Individual differences and personality (15). In everyday speech, people are often described as having 'a lot of personality'. Psychologists use the word 'personality' in a less value-laden sense, to refer to the relatively stable features of a person's behaviour which distinguish him or her from others; thus everyone has a personality and it makes no sense to say that one person has more personality than another. Even very young infants display individual personality differences: some are active while others are passive, some are attentive while others are distractable, and so forth. A personality trait which has attracted a great deal of research attention is extraversion-introversion; extraverts have been shown to differ from introverts in many other significant ways. Self-esteem is another important personality trait: people vary considerably in levels of self-esteem, and an individual's self-esteem often provides a key to understanding other aspects of his or her psychological make-up. In studying individual differences and personality, considerable use is made of psychometrics (see Chapter 1), including standardized tests of intelligence, interests, attitudes, and a wide range of personality traits.

7. Psychopathology (15, 16, 17). Research in this area is

79

concerned with the etiology (origins), symptoms, and treatment of psychological disorders of all kinds. Five major categories of disorders are generally recognized. (a) Mental retardation: a relatively low level of ability to learn, to solve problems, to adapt to new situations, and to think abstractly. (b) Organic psychoses: severe psychological disorders caused by brain damage through disease or injury. (c) Functional psychoses: severe disturbances not associated with any known physical disease or injury. One of the major functional psychoses is schizophrenia, characterized by personality disintegration and abnormalities in behavioural, cognitive, and emotional functioning, and a withdrawal from human contact and reality. Manic-depressive psychosis, which involves dramatic mood-swings, and paranoid states, which are marked by delusions (false beliefs) of persecution, grandeur, and the like, also fall into this category. (d) Neuroses: strong anxiety states, without gross distortion of reality or personality disorganization, experienced in situations not normally considered threatening. Anxiety neurotics experience panic reactions which are not restricted to any particular kinds of situations. Phobics display extreme levels of anxiety when confronted with specific objects or situations, such as strangers (xenophobia), closed spaces (claustrophobia), or thunderstorms (astraphobia), although they recognize that their fears are irrational. Obsessive-compulsives ruminate continuously on certain ideas (obsessions), or repeatedly perform ritual behaviours (compulsions) such as hand-washing, without wishing to think or act in these ways. Hysterics experience blindness, deafness, numbness, or paralyses in the absence of any physical disorders, or losses of memory occasionally associated with alternations between two or more distinct personalities. Neurotic depressives experience exaggerated and usually prolonged reactions to upsetting events. (e) Personality disorders: deeply ingrained maladaptive patterns of behaviour. One of the major types of personality disorder is psychopathy; a psychopath is a frequently dangerous and irresponsible though superficially charming person, lacking the normal ability to distinguish right from wrong, and apparently unable to profit from experience or to give or receive genuine affection. Other disorders usually placed in this category include 'sexual deviations', alcoholism, and drug dependence. Examples of the treatment of various categories of psychological disorders are given in Chapter 6.

8. Developmental psychology (4, 15). This area of research is concerned with psychological phenomena of all kinds in infants and children, and the way they change with age. Since all psychological processes involve developmental changes, research in this area cuts across the categories listed above. Particular attention is, however, given to developmental changes in thinking. This emphasis is no doubt due in part to the great influence of the Swiss developmental psychologist, Jean Piaget, who concentrated on thought processes in children of various ages. A considerable amount of research is also devoted to the effects of various child-rearing practices on later development, to the acquisition of language and moral attitudes in children, to the influences of heredity and environment on the growth of intelligence and personality, and to various other aspects of development from conception to old age.

9. Physiological psychology (1, 2, 3, 9, 11). Research in this area can be divided into two broad categories. Psychophysiology centres on the bodily processes which accompany all of the psychological phenomena outlined in Sections 1-7 above. In particular, important contributions are made by physiological psychologists to understanding states of awareness, learning, sensation and perception, and motivation and emotion. Neuropsychology is concerned with the psychological effects of physical causes such as brain lesions and drugs. Although it deals with physical mechanisms of astonishing complexity — the brain alone contains some thousands of millions of nerve cells and a much larger number of interconnections between them — research in physiological psychology is able to produce many important findings which throw light on psychological phenomena.

10. Social psychology (12, 16, 18, 19, 20). Like developmental and physiological psychology, a large part of social psychology is concerned with investigating all kinds of psychological phenomena from a particular angle; in this case attention focusses on the influences of social factors. But some of the phenomena which are investigated in this area of research are inherently social in character and are not found in individuals; these topics therefore fall exclusively within the domain of social psychology. Examples of the phenomena dealt with in this area are conformity and obedience, attitudes and opinions, group decision-making, non-verbal communication, and interpersonal attraction.

The aims of psychology have been discussed, and an outline has been given of the major areas of psychological research. Taken in conjunction with the detailed examples given in Chapter 2, this should provide a reasonably clear idea of the subject matter of psychology. In order to complete the picture, it is necessary to discuss the methods of research used by psychologists.

Controlled Experiments

Controlled experimentation is the most important research method, and also the most widely misunderstood. Its importance has nothing to do with objectivity (non-experimental methods can be equally objective) or precision (precise measurements are often made in non-experimental investigations) or special instruments (instrumentation is irrelevant to the logic of experimentation). Controlled experimentation is uniquely important for the following reason: it enables conclusions about cause-and-effect relationships to be drawn with a degree of confidence which is not justified when other research methods are used. More than half of the questions given in Chapter 2 were based on the findings of experimental research; Questions 6 through 14 provide particularly clear examples.

The essential features of the experimental method are *manipulation* and *control.* The idea behind manipulation can be explained quite simply. Passive observation often suggests that certain kinds of events are related to one another in a causal manner, but the *reasons* for such relationships cannot be discovered in this way. In order to explain an observed relationship, it is necessary to make a conjecture about the direction of causation and then to test the conjecture by means of an experiment. The experimenter independently manipulates the conjectured causes, which are therefore called *independent variables,* and observes the effects, called *dependent variables.* The need for manipulating independent variables in order to disentangle cause-effect relationships was made explicit for the first time by John Stuart Mill in the nineteenth century. Mill pointed out that we cannot infer that one thing causes another by passively observing the regularity with which the first is followed by the second; this method would lead us to conclude not only that day causes night, but also that night causes day, a conclusion which is not warranted; correlation does not necessarily imply causation. For the same reason, we cannot conclude that drinking alcohol or watching violent television programmes makes people behave aggressively merely by passively observing the aggressive behaviour which often follows these presumed causes. If they are correlated with aggression, this may be because aggressive people are more prone than others to watch violent television programmes and to drink alcohol, or because all three types of behaviour are caused by some underlying factor such as emotional stress. Questions like these are best investigated by controlled experiments, although there is no guarantee that even experimental methods will provide conclusive answers.

The use of control in experimental research can be illustrated with a simple example based on the gas laws in physics. Boyle's law predicts that if the volume of a given mass of gas is decreased — if it is squeezed into a smaller space — then its pressure will increase proportionally. Charles's law predicts that if the temperature of a given mass of gas is increased, then its pressure will increase proportionally. Now the important point emerges that it is impossible to test either of these laws empirically without controlling one of the variables while manipulating another. To test Boyle's law, an experimenter can manipulate the independent variable (the volume of the gas) and observe the effect of this manipulation on the dependent variable (pressure); but no firm conclusions can be drawn from such an investigation unless the irrelevant variable (the temperature of the gas) is held constant. Similarly, Charles's law can be tested only by manipulating the independent variable (temperature) and observing the dependent variable (pressure) while holding constant the irrelevant variable (volume).

In a properly controlled experiment, all irrelevant variables are held constant while the independent variable is manipulated; this is the only way of ensuring that any effects which are observed in the dependent variable can safely be attributed to the independent variable. In the case of the gas laws, experimental control is fairly straightforward because the pressure of a fixed mass of gas is more or less completely accounted for by two variables — volume and temperature — so that only one irrelevant variable needs to be controlled while the independent variable is manipulated. In some psychological experiments, such as those concerned with auditory and visual illusions (see Chapter 2, Questions 9 and 11), simple and direct methods of control can be used in a similar way.

In studying the relative effects of nature and nurture on individual differences and personality, psychologists capitalize on 'experiments of nature' arising from the phenomenon of identical twins. Identical twins are formed when a single egg is fertilized by a single sperm and then divides in two. They are therefore always of the same sex and identical in all other ways which depend entirely on heredity. Since they share all their genes in common, any differences between them, including psychological differences, must be due entirely to environmental causes. Investigations of identical twins reared in different environments are especially useful for estimating the relative importance of genetic and environmental factors. Such investigations involve a high degree of control, since all genetic factors are held constant, but they are not strictly experimental because the manipulation of the independent variable (environment) is done by Mother Nature rather than by the experimenter.

The problems of control in most psychological experiments cannot be dealt with by direct methods. The irrelevant variables which need to be controlled are usually numerous and partly unknown to the investigator, and it is impossible to hold them constant. This difficulty stems partly from the existence of individual differences between people. One litre of oxygen is exactly like any other, and they all respond in exactly the same way when compressed or heated; but no two people — not even identical twins — are alike in all respects, and they do not respond in exactly the same way to similar treatments of all kinds. This fact may seem, on the face of it, to rule out the possibility of experimental control in most areas of psychological research. But in fact it does not: irrelevant variables can be controlled with absolute rigour through indirect methods. This can be most easily explained in terms of a hypothetical example.

Suppose we wish to discover which of two methods of teaching children a foreign language is more effective: a method based on examples only, or one which makes use of both examples and grammatical rules. Assuming that some suitable test is at hand with which we can assess a child's knowledge of the foreign language, how ought we to proceed?

A straightforward approach would be to seek out a number of children who have been taught the foreign language by the examples-only method, and a number who have been exposed to the examples-plus-rules method. We may then simply apply the test to each of the children and compare the average performance of these two groups on it. The problem with this seemingly sensible but non-experimental approach is that the results could not be interpreted in a way which would give a clear answer to the question in hand. This arises from the failure of the research design to control irrelevant variables. If one of the groups turned out to have a higher average test score than the other, this *may* be a consequence of the different teaching methods used, but it may result from one or more of the uncontrolled irrelevant variables. The children in one of the groups may, for example, be more intelligent than those in the other, and this may account for the difference in test scores.

It is not an insuperable problem to control for intelligence, of course. We could simply hold intelligence constant by taking care to match the two groups at the outset according to IQ. If the difference between the groups on the foreign language test emerged even after controlling for intelligence in this way, we may feel more confident in arguing that it is explained by the different teaching methods used. But the weakness of this argument emerges as soon as we realize that there are further possible irrelevant variables to be considered. The problem is much more complex than the one discussed in connection with the gas laws in physics, where only one irrelevant variable had to be taken into account. One of the groups may contain a larger proportion of children whose parents have some knowledge of the foreign language, for example, or the groups may not be equal in terms of the average age of the children. Parents' knowledge of the language, children's age, and other factors may influence the test results. The rather daunting fact has to be faced that there is a potentially infinite list of irrelevant variables which might play a part in determining a child's performance on the foreign language test. Some of them could no doubt be controlled by appropriate matching procedures, but others may be difficult or impossible to control with any accuracy. More seriously still, there may be important factors which affect a child's test performance of which we are simply unaware. We could therefore never be certain that we had controlled all possible irrelevant variables, and we could not conclude from the results of this type of investigation that one or other of the teaching methods is more effective.

An astonishingly simple yet logically compelling solution to this problem was discovered by the British statistician, Ronald A. Fisher, in the early part of this century. The solution is called *randomized experimentation.* The method of procedure is as follows. We begin by selecting a group of children representative of the population to which we wish to generalize our results. We then assign each of these children to one of two treatment conditions strictly at random, by repeatedly tossing a coin for example. The two groups are then treated in exactly the same way, apart from the single difference due to the manipulation of the independent variable, namely that one group is taught the foreign language using the examples-only method while the other is taught by means of the examples-plus-rules method. The dependent variable test is then applied to each child, and the average results of the two groups are compared.

The unexpected power of this type of experimental design derives from the almost miraculous way in which randomization controls at one stroke for the effects of *all possible* irrelevant variables. It has the effect of controlling for IQ, parents' knowledge of the foreign language, children's age, and all conceivable irrelevant variables together with ones which the investigator has not even considered. Randomization does not guarantee an exact matching of the two groups on all these characteristics, but it ensures that they will differ from each other on any one of them at no more than a chance level. The larger the groups, the smaller these chance differences will be, and the more closely the groups will resemble each other in all ways apart from the deliberately manipulated independent variable (teaching methods) and its effects. This can easily be demonstrated with a set of names and addresses selected from a telephone directory. They need not be selected randomly in the first place — any method of selection will do; but if each item is assigned to one of two groups by tossing a coin, the groups will tend to resemble each other on any characteristic whatever, and the resemblance will increase with the size of the groups. The number of two-syllable names, the number of Smiths, the number of addresses in any specified sector of the city, the number of names ending in -w, and the average age, sex, income, education, or any other characteristic of the people listed which one may care to examine, will be found to be approximately equally distributed between the two groups; this approximation will be very close if the groups are large. Any differences which are observed will be due entirely to chance, and they will tend to be small because of the way in which chance operates, as the reader can verify by performing the experiment.

Assigning children at random to the two treatment conditions therefore ensures that all irrelevant variables are controlled and are distributed strictly according to the laws of chance. Now if the groups are treated alike apart from the different teaching methods to which they are exposed, then any difference which is found in their average test scores must be due to the independent variable (teaching methods) or to chance; but the likelihood that any observed difference is due to chance decreases as the size of the groups increases. Of course the possibility of chance differences is never completely ruled out by this method: even if 1000 items from a telephone directory are assigned to two groups at random, the (very small) possibility remains that all of the two-syllable names will end up in one group. This is why statistical methods are necessary for the interpretation of the results of randomized experiments. Statistical tests have been devised for the express purpose of calculating how likely a given set of results is on the basis of chance alone. By applying an appropriate statistical test to the results of our experiment on foreign language teaching, we could decide whether or not it is reasonable to conclude that an observed difference in test scores is due to the greater effectiveness of one or other of the teaching methods used. A detailed discussion of the logic of statistical analysis will be found in Chapter 4.

Controlled experimentation is the most powerful research method available to psychologists, but it does not automatically eliminate all problems of interpretation. If an experiment is well designed, then the *internal validity* of its findings will also be high; this simply means that the conclusions drawn from the results will be true within the limits of the particular subjects and methods used. The experiment on language teaching described above may have high internal validity, but nevertheless lack *external validity*: the results may be valid only for the kinds of children, teachers, and language tests used in the experiment. One teaching method may, for example, turn out to be more effective than another although a different result would have emerged if children of a higher average ability level, or teachers with more progressive attitudes, or a different measure of attainment had been used. In order to establish the external validity of the findings, it is usually necessary to replicate the experiment with different subjects and under different conditions. The problem then remains of the *ecological validity* of the findings: the confidence with which they may be generalized to natural (non-experimental) situations in which children learn foreign languages. Many of these problems can be dealt with to an extent by judiciously chosen research designs and procedures, but the reader should appreciate that all sorts of complications which have not been touched upon arise in controlled experimentation: large volumes have been filled with discussions of elaborate experimental designs and procedures.

Before leaving the topic of controlled experimentation, it is worth mentioning the distinction between laboratory and field experiments. Most experiments in psychology are conducted under laboratory conditions, in which extraneous stimuli are most easily excluded and proper procedures of manipulation and control are most conveniently carried out. On-line computers or microprocessors and other items of equipment are often used for manipulating independent variables and measuring dependent variables in the most efficient ways. In some cases, however, it is both desirable and possible to conduct controlled experiments in natural settings, and such investigations are often called field experiments. All of the experiments described in Chapter 2 were laboratory experiments, but a field experiment in an ordinary school could be used to examine the relative effectiveness of teaching methods in the example described above. Field experiments are quite frequently used in some areas of psychological research, particularly social psychology. They usually raise difficult problems of manipulation and control, but they have the compensating advantage of high ecological validity.

Quasi-experiments

For one reason or another, many questions about causal relationships which crop up in psychology do not lend themselves to strictly experimental methods of investigation. In these cases the conjectured causes cannot be manipulated directly; or, to put it differently, the independent variable cannot be varied independently. A consequence of this is that irrelevant variables can be controlled neither directly nor by indirect methods of randomization. The research designs which are used for investigating questions like these are called *quasi-experiments*. They resemble controlled experiments in so far as they centre on relationships between conjectured causes and effects, but they lack the manipulation and control procedures characteristic of strictly experimental designs.

A typical example of quasi-experimentation was discussed in Chapter 2 (Question 4) in connection with the effects of age on ability to solve problems involving conservation of substance. The problem of research design in that case is as follows: The critical factor is assumed to be the level of cognitive development which in turn depends largely upon age. But young children differ from adolescents and adults in countless ways apart from age-dependent level of cognitive development; they tend, for example, to be less well educated. It is impossible for an investigator to hold education and all other irrelevant variables constant while comparing the thought processes of people of different ages. There is no way in which people can be randomly assigned to different age levels. But a systematic comparison can nevertheless be made between the thought processes of children in carefully specified age ranges, through the use of standardized tests of conservation ability. In other words, quasi-experimental methods can be used. The results of quasi-experiments are in general not as unambiguous as those of controlled experiments, and they need to be interpreted with caution. In many cases, including Piaget's conservation studies, common sense bids us to accept the findings as valid — the failure of young children on conservation tasks seems likely to be due to cognitive immaturity — but in other cases serious problems of interpretation arise.

A notorious example revolves around the interpretation of quasi-experimental investigations of differences in intelligence between certain ethnic groups, notably black and white Americans. Numerous studies have shown that black Americans score, on average, approximately 15 points below their white compatriots on standardized IQ tests. Some psychologists are anxious to argue that this finding is largely due to genetic differences between the two groups, while others claim that it can be accounted for by a multitude of cultural factors. In order to examine the influence of genetic factors experimentally, it would be necessary to assign sets of 'black' and 'white' genes to a group of infants, to expose them to identical environmental conditions for a number of years, and then to measure their IQs. Since such a controlled experiment is manifestly impossible to carry out, ideological considerations tend to dominate interpretations of the existing evidence on this question.

In quasi-experimental research, it is sometimes possible to 'control' one or more (but not all) of the irrelevant variables by statistical methods after the data have been collected. An instructive and simple example occurred in a recent investigation of the personality characteristics of women who develop breast cancer. A group of 160 women with breast tumours were interviewed and given a number of personality tests on the day before they underwent operations to discover whether or not their tumours were malignant (cancerous). At the time of testing, neither the subjects nor the investigators knew which tumours were malignant. After the operation, 69 women were found to have breast cancer and 91 were found to have non-malignant tumours. The investigators then compared the psychological data relating to these two groups. The most significant findings centred on the women's characteristic mode of expressing anger. Among the 'extreme suppressors' who virtually never expressed anger openly, and the 'extreme expressors' who had a history of frequent outbursts of temper, 67 per cent had malignant tumours, while among the women who expressed anger 'normally', only 23 per cent of the tumours were malignant. Statistical analysis (see Chapter 4) showed that a difference as large as this is extremely unlikely on the basis of chance alone; in other words, the results are statistically significant.

Do they suggest a causal link between personality and breast cancer? Since the research design was quasi-experimental, such a conclusion is not justified; the results may arise from any number of uncontrolled irrelevant variables. In fact the investigators anticipated this criticism and examined one of the more obvious irrelevant variables, namely the ages of the women. The women whose tumours were malignant turned out to be older, on average, than the women with non-malignant tumours. This implies that the relationship between personality and breast cancer may be entirely due to age: as women get older, they may become more extreme in their manner of expressing anger, and may also be more likely to develop breast cancer. The investigators therefore 'controlled' for age by re-analysing the results separately for women in various age groups. The findings remained statistically significant even when the effects of age were controlled in this way. But they are by no means conclusive in demonstrating a causal link between personality and breast cancer, because other (unknown and uncontrolled) variables were not ruled out by the research design.

Quasi-experiments do not in general produce findings with the same degree of internal (and therefore also external and ecological) validity as controlled experiments. In some cases, the results are simply uninterpretable. In others, the relative weakness of the research design is less troublesome, and reasonably firm conclusions can be justified on common-sense grounds. In any event, psychologists have to learn to live with this research method whether they like it or not, because conjectures about causal relationships often need to be tested in circumstances where manipulation and control are not feasible.

Survey Methods

The aim of survey research in psychology is to investigate factors of psychological interest in specific sections of a population or in different populations. Investigations which focus on comparisons between different cultural groups are called *cross-cultural surveys*. Surveys which are confined to single populations usually investigate differences between groups defined according to demographic variables such as geographical location, ethnic identity, age, sex, social class, marital status, and education. Question 16 in Chapter 2, for example, was based upon surveys of the distribution of psychological disorders across the social class hierarchy in various industrial societies. Survey methods are normally used to answer specific questions about the prevalence of opinions, attitudes, beliefs, personality characteristics, psychological disorders, and behaviour patterns among large population groups, and they raise special problems of research design and methodology.

The most difficult problem in survey research concerns methods of sampling. The investigator needs to ensure that the individuals studied are properly representative of the population groups to which they belong, otherwise the findings will not be generalizable and the survey will lack external validity. If the population is not too large, it is occasionally possible to carry out a *census* survey in which every single member of the population is examined. This method was used by Hollingshead and Redlich in their survey of the psychiatric patients in New Haven described in the answer to Question 16 in Chapter 2. Usually, however, it is necessary to restrict the investigation to a small proportion of the population, and this raises the problem of sampling.

The ideal method of sampling, from a theoretical point of view, is *simple random sampling,* in which the investigator selects a number of individuals strictly at random from the population. This technique ensures that every member of the population has an equal chance of being included in the sample, and if the sample is reasonably large, then it will be unbiased with regard to social class, age, sex, and all other imagined and unimagined population variables; in other words it will be truly representative. Simple random sampling is, however, not used very often because of the difficulty of drawing up a list of all members of the population — a *sampling frame* — from which the random selection can be made. Voter registration lists are sometimes used, but they tend to omit certain sections of the population and become out of date very rapidly. Telephone directories may be used as sampling frames for some purposes, but households at both extremes of the social hierarchy tend to be under-represented (though for different reasons) when samples are drawn in this way. To counter these problems, *stratified random sampling* is sometimes used. This is a random sampling technique applied piecewise to each stratum of the population. It is designed to ensure that all sections of the population are adequately represented in the sample.

In practice, simple, stratified, and other random sampling procedures are expensive, difficult, and unsatisfactory for a number of other reasons. They seldom produce samples which are truly random or representative because certain categories of people are more likely than others to refuse to participate in surveys. The technique which is therefore most commonly used, not only by psychological survey researchers but also by market research and opinion polling organizations, is *quota sampling*: individuals are selected in a hit-and-miss fashion until the sample contains a predetermined quota in each of a number of categories usually reflecting their proportions in the population at large. In many cases, quota sampling is no less reliable than random sampling, and it is a good deal cheaper and easier to carry out. It seems to work quite well in practice.

Having selected a suitable sample, the next problem confronting a survey researcher is to extract the required information from it. The most common sources of information are interviews and questionnaires.

Interviews are relatively easy to use, but the information derived from them is subject to various subtle forms of bias. Minute and seemingly insignificant variations in the phrasing of questions sometimes have dramatic effects on the way in which they are answered. Survey researchers have learned through bitter experience that people's answers to certain kinds of questions simply cannot be taken at face value. In a survey of attitudes towards organized religion, for example, an interviewee may answer 'Yes' to the straightforward question 'Are you in favour of organized religion?' for any one of a number of reasons, including the following: (a) because he is strongly in favour of organized religion; (b) because he is slightly in favour of organized religion; (c) because he thinks he will give a better impression of himself by answering 'Yes' than by answering 'No'; (d) because of a tendency known as *acquiescence response set* in many people to answer 'Yes' to most questions which are put to them; (e) because he answered 'No' to several previous questions and wants to introduce some variety into his answers; (f) because he thinks the interviewer wants him to answer 'Yes'.

A great deal is known about how people answer questions, and some of the problems of interviews can be overcome or reduced by the use of questionnaires. A properly constructed questionnaire is an objective measuring instrument whose validity has been carefully checked by determining how successfully it discriminates in practice between known criterion groups. In checking the validity of a questionnaire to measure attitudes towards organized religion, for example, the criterion groups might be regular church attenders and atheists. Sophisticated techniques are available for constructing questionnaires so that they have maximum discriminating power and other desirable characteristics. Acquiescence response set, for example, can be taken care of by wording half of the items in the questionnaire so that a 'Yes' answer represents an attitude in favour of the issue in question, like the question mentioned earlier, and the other half so that a 'Yes' answer represents an attitude against it (eg 'Do you believe that organized religion is a waste of time?'); this ensures that acquiescence response set will not bias the respondent's overall score in one direction or the other. Although elaborate questionnaires of this type are extremely valuable in surveys devoted to subtle attitudes and personality traits, they are not always necessary, particularly when the research focusses on gross behavioural differences between population groups.

Ethological Investigations

Ethological methods originated in zoology and became prominent in the 1930s with the work of Konrad Lorenz. They involve careful observations of the behaviour of animals and people in their natural habitats. In contrast with survey methods, ethological investigations are based upon naturalistic observations; the ethologist simply describes the observed behaviour and refrains as far as possible from intervening in the situation in a way which might influence it in any way. Ethological investigations tend to be less narrowly focussed on providing answers to specific questions than other methods of investigation; they are generally more exploratory in spirit. The answer to Question 19 in Chapter 2 was based partly on the findings of ethological investigations of sexual behaviour in various cultures. Ethological methods have recently become quite common in certain areas of psychological research, notably in various branches of social and developmental psychology.

A branch of social psychology which illustrates the uses of ethological methods is the study of *proxemics,* or the spatial features of human social interaction. Investigations in this area have revealed surprisingly strict — though largely unconscious — social conventions governing the use of personal space. Ethological studies have shown that the optimal nose-to-nose distance for ordinary conversations in the United States and Northern European cultures is 30 to 48 inches (76 to 122 centimetres). Even quite small deviations beyond these limits in either direction have been observed to lead to visible signs of discomfort and efforts to re-establish conventional distances. Other cultures have different — though equally rigid — proxemic conventions. Arab cultures, for example, prescribe much closer interpersonal distances, so that when an Arab talks to an American, the Arab may keep advancing while the American keeps retreating, and both may feel uncomfortable. Ethological

investigations have also revealed that cultures which prescribe close interpersonal distances usually allow more body contact between relative strangers than do the 'non-contact' cultures of the United States and Northern Europe.

Ethological research sometimes suggests cause-and-effect relationships between variables, although for reasons explained above experimental methods are necessary to corroborate them. Both methods of research, for example, have generated findings about the effects of invasions of personal space. The voluntary narrowing of interpersonal distance usually communicates an attempt to raise the level of intimacy of an interaction. The appropriate distance for intimate conversations in non-contact cultures is about 6 to 18 inches (15 to 46 centimetres), and if both parties agree that the interaction is intimate they will not feel uncomfortable at this distance and may even try to diminish it further. But if one of the parties does not agree with this implied definition of the situation, he or she usually tries to increase the distance or, failing that, to reduce the level of intimacy conveyed by other non-verbal signals such as voice quality, facial expression, and eye contact, in order to compensate for the excessively close physical proximity. Intimacy-reducing manoeuvres like these have been observed in ethological investigations in crowded lifts, underground trains, and other environments of enforced closeness.

The range of psychological phenomena which can be investigated through ethological methods is rather limited, but where they can be used they often provide illuminating findings. Since the techniques of recording behaviour are often largely informal and unsystematic, however, the findings sometimes raise problems of internal and external validity: different observers may describe the same behaviour in quite different ways which suggest widely divergent interpretations. Problems of ecological validity, on the other hand, are virtually absent when ethological methods are used.

Case Studies

A psychological case study is a detailed investigation of a single person. Investigations of this type are extensively used in clinical psychology; they usually take the form of detailed descriptions of individuals manifesting unusual psychological disorders or brain lesions, or their responses to particular methods of treatment. In other areas of psychology they are less common, but they are sometimes used for studying individuals who have undergone unusual experiences which might have interesting psychological consequences. The detailed investigation of S.B. following his recovery from life-long blindness, described in the answer to Question 5 in Chapter 2, is a typical case which falls into this category. The data which are reported in case studies come from various sources, including interviews, written records, questionnaires and other psychometric tests, and direct observations of behaviour.

An instructive example of the use of a case study concerns Freud's theory of paranoia. Paranoia is a psychological disorder marked by delusions of various kinds. Freud noted that the following categories of delusions were most common among the paranoiacs whom he had seen in his clinical practice: (a) jealousy: paranoiacs frequently make unfounded accusations of unfaithfulness against their spouses or lovers; (b) erotomania: some paranoiacs suffer from the delusion that numerous members of the opposite sex are in love with them; (c) persecution: paranoiacs often imagine plots to kill or harm them; (d) grandeur: many paranoiacs believe themselves to be gods or emperors, or beings of great power and importance.

The following question arises: Why are the delusions of paranoiacs usually of these types? What is special about these delusions? In an extremely penetrating case study based upon the memoirs of a High Court Judge called Schreber who suffered from paranoia for many years, Freud came to the conclusion that an unconscious homosexual wish-fantasy lies at the root of the paranoid disorder and explains the types of delusions which characterize it. The unconscious wish-fantasy may be expressed in the following sentence: *I (a man) love him (a man).*

Since homosexuality is socially taboo, the paranoiac strives unconsciously to distort the wish-fantasy to prevent himself from having to confront it at a conscious level. He may first of all distort the grammatical subject of the sentence by a psychological defence mechanism called *projection,* that is by attributing his own unconscious desires to someone else. The distorted version is then: *It is not I, but she (my spouse), who loves him,* and delusions of jealousy arise. Or he may distort the object of the sentence: *It is impossible that I should love a man; I love numerous women.* In this form, the wish-fantasy is still unacceptable (at least to a Victorian married man), and is thus further distorted by projection into the form: *Numerous women love me,* and delusions of erotomania arise. The paranoiac may also distort the verb of the sentence by turning it around: *I do not love a man; I hate men.* But, once again, since it is unacceptable to hate people for no good reason, this version has to be further distorted by projection into the form: *Men hate me,* and delusions of persecution arise. Finally, the paranoiac may deny the entire sentence: *I do not love a man; I love no one.* But sexual energy cannot evaporate into thin air, according to Freud, so this statement is equivalent to the following: *I love no one but myself,* which accounts for delusions of grandeur. All of the common categories of paranoiac delusions are therefore explained in terms of the homosexual wish-fantasy which Freud uncovered in his case study of Herr Schreber.

In spite of its logical elegance and explanatory power, Freud's theory of paranoia is not accepted by all clinical psychologists, or even by all psychoanalysts. Nonetheless, the detailed account given above illustrates the extremely ambitious aims which case studies can sometimes serve. The aims are, of course, usually more modest than this. But provided that it is reasonable to assume that what is true of the individual case is also true of a larger class of people — a condition which is often met — the findings of case studies can provide important insights into psychological phenomena.

Further Reading

One of the best introductions to research methodology is Festinger, L. and Katz, D. (eds.), *Research Methods in the Behavioral Sciences* (New York: Holt, Rinehart and Winston, 1953). The logic of randomized experimentation and associated data analysis was originally worked out by

R.A. Fisher, whose *The Design of Experiments*, 4th ed. (London: Oliver and Boyd, 1947) is a classic of lucid exposition. A detailed discussion of the most widely used research methods is given by D.T. Campbell and J.C. Stanley in *Experimental and Quasi-experimental Designs for Research* (Chicago: Rand McNally, 1966), and an authoritative and up-to-date treatment of controlled experimentation, quasi-experimentation, survey methods, and ethological investigations (which the authors call 'passive observational studies') is given by T.D. Cook and D.T. Campbell in *Quasi-experimentation: Design and Analysis Issues for Field Settings* (Chicago: Rand McNally, 1979). The latter two works deal with a wider range of research methods than their titles suggest, though both arbitrarily restrict the definition of controlled experimentation to investigations in which randomization is used.

The investigation of personality characteristics among women who develop breast cancer referred to in this chapter was reported by S. Greer and T. Morris in a paper entitled 'Psychological attributes of women who develop breast cancer: a controlled study' (*Journal of Psychosomatic Research*, 1975, **19**, 147-53). The original case study in which Freud developed his theory of paranoia can be found in his *Collected Papers*, authorized and translated by A. and J. Strachey, Volume III (London: Hogarth, 1948, pp 387-470).

4. Statistical Methods

People are often surprised to discover that statistics has any part to play in psychology. Some are positively alarmed by the discovery, and abandon all thought of studying psychology for this sole reason. In fact, the level of statistical ability which is absolutely essential for psychologists is very low, and there are few who cannot easily master the basic skills. Professional psychologists, for their part, vary widely in their understanding of statistics. Many, particularly among those with arts rather than science backgrounds, get by with only a rudimentary grasp of the fundamental ideas; this enables them to apply a handful of simple statistical tests to standard types of problems in a more or less mechanical way. They accept on trust that these tests do what they are supposed to do, and when they are faced with problems which cannot be solved by routine methods, they simply seek advice from their more numerate colleagues.

An elementary knowledge of statistics is indispensable for making sense of the technical literature of psychology, because research findings are nearly always reported in numerical form and analysed by statistical methods. There are two reasons for this. The first is that statistical techniques are available for summarizing data in the most compact and unambiguous ways. This rather dry branch of statistics is called *descriptive statistics*. It is devoted to methods of presenting numerical data in tables or graphs, and of calculating averages, variabilities, correlations, and so forth. Statistics of this kind is familiar to most people in phrases like 'unemployment statistics', 'trade statistics', and 'accident statistics'. Descriptive statistics has been used for presenting psychological data ever since the 1860s when the British psychologist, Francis Galton, first used it for describing the results of his investigations of intelligence (see Chapter 5).

The second reason why statistics is used in psychology is more subtle and much more important. It concerns the problem of *interpreting* data. This problem arises whenever, as is usually the case, the data are not quite clear-cut or, to put it another way, when they do not 'speak for themselves'. A second major branch of statistics, called *inferential statistics*, comes to our aid in these cases. Inferential statistics reached maturity only in the 1930s, largely as a result of the work of the British statistician Ronald A. Fisher. It is devoted entirely to methods of drawing *inferences* from samples of numerical data. The main purpose of inferential statistics is most easily explained in terms of a hypothetical example.

Let us suppose that an experiment like the one described in Chapter 3 has been performed in order to discover which of two methods is more effective in teaching children a foreign language. A possible set of results is shown in Table 1.

Scores (out of 20) on Criterion Test

Group taught by examples only	10	15	14	8	9	14	6	7	11	13
Group taught by examples plus rules	11	17	14	10	11	15	10	8	12	15

Table 1: *Effectiveness of two teaching methods*

The first group does not seem to have done quite as well as the second. The average scores are 10.7 and 12.3 respectively. The scores of the second group look distinctly higher than those of the first. But what conclusion can be drawn from these results? One would obviously not expect the two groups to obtain identical scores even if the teaching methods were equally effective, because other (extraneous) factors, such as differences between the children in age, intelligence, motivation and so forth are bound to have affected their test scores. But we know that these extraneous factors are randomly distributed between the two groups, because an experimental design was used and the children were thus assigned to the two treatment conditions strictly at random (see Chapter 3). All differences between the scores must result either from such randomly distributed extraneous factors, or from the differences in teaching methods, or both.

The fact that the children were randomly assigned to treatment conditions does not, of course, guarantee that all the extraneous factors which influenced their test scores are *equally* distributed between the two groups. What it does guarantee, however, is that the distribution obeys the laws of chance. The question which needs to be answered is this: Is the higher average score of the children in the second group due entirely to chance, that is, to the uneven distribution of extraneous factors between the two groups? Or is it due to the different methods of instruction? Would it be prudent to conclude from these figures that the examples-plus-rules method of instruction is definitely superior to the examples-only method? The answer, as it happens, is no. The likelihood of finding a difference as large as this on the basis of chance alone is in fact in the region of one in four. This result is obtained by the straightforward application of a simple and well-known statistical technique called the *t* test. Special techniques of this type are needed for interpreting data because, without them, people are apt to interpret results incorrectly or to find themselves at a loss to interpret them at all. The human mind, astonishingly powerful though it is at many kinds of tasks, is, as we shall see, very poor at estimating likelihoods.

The results of most psychological investigations are analysed by means of a small number of well known statistical tests which are versatile and powerful yet easy to apply. The calculations are nowadays usually done by computers, for which packages of standard statistical tests are available as software. For these reasons, a little knowledge of statistics goes a long way in psychology. But a little knowledge can also, as our elders and betters never tire of reminding us, be a dangerous thing. The mechanical and unquestioning approach to statistics sometimes leads to serious errors, and it fails completely with data which do not conveniently fit the standard tests. An understanding of the ideas which lie behind the tests is therefore highly desirable. A clear insight into the theory of statistics enables all problems of analysis to be approached with confidence and safety. It has the added advantage of revealing the unexpected charm and fascination of statistical ideas.

In this chapter, therefore, I shall not attempt to provide a survey of all the statistical tests which are commonly used in psychology. The more ambitious aim is to convey the essential underlying ideas of statistical theory through a complete analysis, from first principles, of a real set of psychological data and a few supplementary problems. The fundamental ideas are common to all statistical tests, and they are all revealed in these simple examples. The logic of each step in the analyses in explained in detail without assuming any previous knowledge, aside from arithmetic and the most elementary algebra. A much deeper understanding of statistics will be gained by savouring these morsels of analysis than by swallowing any number of pre-digested statistical techniques without any preparation.

A Crime in Jung's Asylum

On February 6, 1908, a theft was reported at an asylum for the insane in Zürich, Switzerland. The facts were as follows. One of the asylum's nurses had left a dark reddish leather purse in a clothes closet in her room. The purse contained a 50-franc note, a 20-franc coin, a few centimes, a silver watch-chain, a stencil used for marking the asylum's kitchen utensils, and a receipt form Dosenbach's Shoe Shop. The purse and its contents had mysteriously disappeared during the afternoon. The circumstances of the theft pointed to three of the nurse's colleagues as prime suspects. Unfortunately for the thief, the incident came to the attention of a member of the asylum's staff, the famous psychiatrist Carl Gustav Jung (1875-1961), who immediately took up the challenge of attempting to solve the crime by using his newly developed word-association test as a lie detector.

Jung proceeded to compose a list of 'critical' words, most of which were associated with intimate details of the crime, such as *watch, chain, leather, dark-reddish, stencil, receipt, Dosenbach, fifty,* and *twenty.* He distributed 37 such critical words evenly among 63 'indifferent stimulus words' which were similar to the critical words except that they had no particular relevance to the crime. The complete list therefore contained 100 words. One may assume that any number of these words may have special emotional significance for a given person, but the validity of Jung's test relies on the assumption that the critical and non-critical words should not differ systematically in emotional significance for an innocent person who had no knowledge of the intimate details of the crime. To put it another way, any tendency to respond differently to the critical and non-critical words to a degree which exceeds chance expectation is assumed to be evidence of guilt.

Following his usual procedure when testing neurotic patients, Jung applied this specially devised word-association test to each of the suspect nurses in turn. The 100 words were read out one by one and the suspect was asked to respond with the first word which came into her mind in each case. Careful note was taken of 'complex indicators' such as abnormally long reaction times, multiple responses, repetitions of the stimulus words, and meaningless associations. The complete list was then read out a second time, and the nurse was asked to try to remember her original responses. Jung considered imperfect reproductions to be further complex indicators of particular importance.

Of the three suspects, A, B and C, only the second reacted to the test in an obviously anxious manner, and her general demeanour spoke strongly against her. Jung commented: 'It seemed to me that she evinced a very "suspicious", or I might almost say, "impudent" countenance. With the idea of finding in her the guilty one I set about adding up the results. . . .One must always resort to calculation, as appearances are enormously deceptive'. Jung's 'calculation' was in reality nothing more than a summary of the data; inferential statistics was still in its infancy in 1908 and appropriate methods of analysis were not available to Jung. Nevertheless, an intuitive interpretation of the data convinced him that Nurse A and not Nurse B was the guilty party, in spite of his earlier suspicions. Nurse A later broke down and made a complete confession. This enabled Jung to comment with obvious satisfaction: 'Thus the success of the experiment was confirmed. . . .There is much in experimental psychology which is less useful that the material treated in this work'.

Type of Word	Nurse A		Nurse B		Nurse C	
	Imperfect	Perfect	Imperfect	Perfect	Imperfect	Perfect
Critical	19	18	9	28	12	25
Non-critical	15	48	19	44	18	45

Table 2: *Imperfect and perfect reproductions among three suspect nurses*

The most incriminating feature of Nurse A's test results was the large number of imperfect reproductions which she gave to the critical words in the list. The distribution of imperfect and perfect reproductions to critical and non-critical words for each of the three suspect nurses is shown in

Table 2.

An examination of these data reveals certain interesting facts. It is clear that all three nurses gave more perfect than imperfect reproductions. Nurse B and Nurse C gave more than twice as many perfect as imperfect reproductions to both critical and non-critical words. Nurse A also gave more than twice as many perfect as imperfect reproductions to the non-critical words, but to the critical words her imperfect reproductions outnumbered her perfect reproductions. In Jung's view, her imperfect reproductions to critical words 'surpass by far the expected' and he concluded that 'practically one may venture to designate such a subject as probably guilty'. But what exactly is to be 'expected'? With how much confidence can we 'designate such a subject as probably guilty' on the basis of these data?

The results of Jung's word-association test seem to show that Nurse A had a stronger tendency to give imperfect reproductions to critical than to non-critical words. But there are numerous extraneous factors which influence a person's responses to a word-association test. In this case we are interested only in whether a knowledge of the intimate details of the crime influenced Nurse A's imperfect reproductions to critical and non-critical words. Other factors which cause imperfect reproductions are presumed to be randomly distributed between the critical and non-critical words; we shall return to this point later.

The question which needs to be answered is this: What is the probability of an innocent person producing a pattern of responses as seemingly incriminating as those of Nurse A on the basis of chance alone? Before rolling out the big guns of inferential statistics to attack this problem, it is necessary to show why such extreme measures are in order. To be specific, it is necessary to convince the reader that special techniques of analysis are needed because informal, 'commonsense' estimates of probability are extremely unreliable and sometimes quite misleading. The discussion which follows will also serve the useful purpose of providing an intuitive background to the notion of probability which lies at the heart of statistics.

Bombs, Horse Kicks and Juries

The following three examples, drawn from widely differing areas of life in which numbers crop up, show how misleading unaided intuition can be in estimating probabilities.

(a) The bombing of London. During the Second World War, London was repeatedly attacked by German bomber aircraft. Many areas were hit several times while many others escaped altogether. An area of South London was hit by 537 bombs. This area can be divided into 576 sectors of a quarter of a square kilometre each in order to show how the bombs were distributed. It turns out that no fewer than 136 of these sectors were each hit more than once, and 229 sectors were never hit; only 211 sectors were each hit exactly once. On intuitive grounds, this pattern may seem distinctly non-random and improbable on the basis of chance alone; most Londoners in fact believed that certain sectors were more at risk from aerial bombardment than others. Statistical methods which are explained later in this chapter may be used to calculate the distribution of hits which would be expected from bombs falling completely at random over this area. Table 3 shows the observed distribution of hits together with the distribution to be expected on the basis of chance alone.

Number of hits	0	1	2	3	4	5 +
Observed number of sectors	229	211	93	35	7	1
Expected number of sectors	227	211	99	31	7	1

Table 3: *Observed and expected distributions of 537 bomb hits over 576 sectors of South London*

The observed and expected distributions show a remarkably close fit. The fact that most Londoners did not believe the bombs were falling at random simply shows what poor intuitive statisticians they were. But in fairness to wartime Londoners it should be pointed out that, even to the unaided eye of a trained statistician, randomness often seems markedly non-random and vice versa.

(b) Deaths from horse kicks. Over a 20-year period from 1875 to 1894, 122 men in 200 Prussian Army Corps died as a result of kicks from horses. Assuming that accidents like this strike purely at random, how might one expect the 122 deaths to be distributed among the 200 corps? The deaths were in fact distributed in what seemed to many people to be an unmistakably non-random pattern. No fewer than 26 of the corps suffered more than one death due to horse kicks, and in

one corps four such misfortunes occurred. These findings played a large part in the development of a spurious and supernatural theory of accident-proneness. A well-known analysis based on statistical methods discussed later in this chapter shows that the pattern of deaths corresponds very closely to the pattern which would be expected on the basis of chance alone. The observed and expected distributions are shown in Table 4.

Number of deaths	0	1	2	3	4
Observed number of corps	109	65	22	3	1
Expected number of corps	109	66	20	4	1

Table 4: *Observed and expected distributions of 122 deaths due to horse kicks among 200 Prussian Army Corps*

The distribution which many people intuitively feel to be most likely on the basis of chance is one death in each of 122 of the 200 corps. The probability of this 'even' distribution is roughly one in 10,000,000,000,000,000,000,000. In other words, it would be a miracle.

(c) Jury verdicts. In the case *Johnson v. Louisiana* in 1972, the United States Supreme Court was asked to decide the following question: Is a 12-member jury which is required to reach a verdict by a majority of at least nine votes to three more or less likely to convict than a five-member jury which has to be unanimous in its verdict? In order to 'facilitate, expedite, and reduce expenses in the administration of criminal justice', Louisiana uses five-member unanimous juries for less serious crimes, and reserves the use of 12-member juries for more serious crimes. In some cases, the larger juries are permitted to convict by a nine-to-three majority. Johnson was convicted of robbery by this majority following an identification parade. He appealed to the Supreme Court and argued that, other things being equal, a five-member unanimous jury was less likely to have convicted him. He claimed that he should have been afforded at least as much protection as a defendant in a less serious case.

The appeal was rejected. The Court analysed the problem as follows: 'Three jurors here voted to acquit, but . . . this does not demonstrate that the appellant was convicted on a lower standard of proof. To obtain a conviction in any of the categories under Louisiana law, the State must prove guilt beyond reasonable doubt, but the number of jurors who must be so convinced increases with the seriousness of the crime . . . If the appellant's position is that it is easier to convince nine of 12 jurors than to convince all of five, he is simply challenging the judgment of the Louisiana Legislature. That body obviously intended to vary the difficulty of proving guilt with the gravity of the offense and the severity of the punishment. We remain unconvinced by anything the appellant has presented that this legislative judgment was defective in any constitutional sense'.

The most direct method of 'simply challenging the judgment of the Louisiana Legislature', and that of the United States Supreme Court as well, is by calculating the probability that Johnson would have been convicted by a five-member unanimous jury drawn at random from among the original 12 jurors. The Court evidently believed that a five-member unanimous jury was more likely to have convicted him than a 12-member jury with a nine-to-three majority. A method of calculation explained later in this chapter is directly applicable here. Assuming each of the jurors in the Johnson case to be firm in his or her vote of guilt or innocence, it turns out that, of all the five-member juries which could be selected from among these 12 jurors, more than 84 per cent would have insufficient votes to convict unanimously. In other words, if one such five-member jury were selected at random from among the original 12 jurors, the probability is less than 0.16 that it would have convicted Johnson.

The three examples discussed above illustrate vividly how unreliable purely intuitive estimates of probability can be. Bearing in mind the necessity for objective probability calculations, we are now ready to embark upon the statistical analysis of Jung's data. We need to calculate the probability that a pattern of responses as seemingly incriminating as that of Nurse A's is due to chance alone. (For simplicity's sake, we shall pretend that Jung tested only Nurse A, although, strictly speaking, the probability of finding an unusual set of responses by chance alone obviously increases with the number of nurses tested.) The solution of statistical problems of this kind always begins with the construction of a suitable *model.* The purposes of the model are to re-formulate the problem more precisely, and to state unambiguously what assumptions have to be made, since certain assumptions are always necessary.

An Urn Model

We need to calculate the probability of a person giving as many as 19 out of 34 imperfect reproductions to critical words in Jung's word-association test on the basis of chance alone. Given that there were 34 imperfect reproductions among Nurse A's responses to the test, how improbable is it, on the basis of chance alone, that as many as 19 of them should be associated with critical words? The probability we are after is not that of *exactly* 19 imperfect reproductions, but that of 19 *or more*. The probability of *any particular* outcome is, of course, very small whether given by a guilty or an innocent person. This tricky point can be clarified with the following example. Suppose 100 animals were injected with a drug, and 80 of them developed an unusual type of tumour. A medical researcher might comment that this is unlikely to be due to chance alone, and that the tumours seem to have been caused by the drug. This is not meant to imply that it is unlikely that *exactly* 80 animals developed the tumours spontaneously, but that it is unlikely that *as many* as 80 (that is, 80 or more) did so. For the same reason, the probability we are seeking is that of 19 *or more* imperfect reproductions to critical words.

The following model clarifies the statistical features of the problem and the assumptions which are built into it. Supposes that an urn contains 100 billiard balls, of which 37 are red and 63 are black. A person is blindfolded and instructed to select any number of the balls at random. If 34 balls are selected in this way, what is the probability that 19 or more of them will be red? In this model, the red balls correspond to the 37 critical words in Jung's list, and the black balls represent the 63 non-critical words. The act of selecting 34 balls represents Nurse A's 34 imperfect reproductions. The manner of selecting the balls — blindfolded and at random — entails two critical assumptions: that Nurse A was innocent, and that the critical and non-critical words are indistinguishable to an innocent person. This implies that her imperfect reproductions were distributed randomly between the critical and non-critical words.

The validity of any statistical calculation depends upon the reasonableness of the model. In this case, we are dealing with imperfect reproductions in a word-association test. There are presumably all manner of factors which cause people to give imperfect reproductions, but we are concerned with only one possible factor, namely the critical nature of some of the words. It is assumed that this factor may cause a guilty person to give more imperfect reproductions to critical than to non-critical words, but that it could have no such effect on an innocent person. Linked to this is the assumption that all other (extraneous) factors which may cause imperfect reproductions are randomly distributed between the critical and non-critical words. Translated into the urn model, this is equivalent to assuming that the red and black balls are indistinguishable to a blindfolded person.

We can check the reasonableness of these assumptions in an informal way by simply examining the words in the list. There were, in fact, certain peculiarities in the way Jung drew up his list, but there are no striking differences between the critical and the non-critical words apart from the association of the former with the crime. It is worth noting also that Nurse B and Nurse C gave approximately the same proportion of imperfect reproductions to critical and to non-critical words, which suggests that the two kinds of words are similar in the eyes of innocent people. But we cannot be sure that these nurses were both innocent, and we do not know, in any event, that what was true for them was necessarily true for Nurse A. The urn model seems reasonable enough, but it entails assumptions which are not absolutely certain. The point is that Jung's research design was, of necessity, quasi-experimental. Only strictly experimental designs can guarantee that all extraneous factors are properly controlled in the sense of being randomly distributed between treatment conditions (see Chapter 3).

The Null Hypothesis

Built into the urn model is one assumption which merits special attention. The assumption is that the selection of balls is made at random by a blindfolded person. This is equivalent to assuming that Nurse A was innocent. An assumption of this kind has a special status in a statistical calculation. It represents what is known as the *null hypothesis.* All the other assumptions in the statistical model are assumed to be true, and the validity of the calculation depends upon their truth. The null hypothesis, on the other hand, is assumed to be true only in a provisional sense. The investigator does not actually *believe* the null hypothesis to be true. The purpose of the calculation is to discover precisely how much confidence we can place in it, given the particular set of data at hand. In the case of Jung's data, we wish to know whether the null hypothesis of blind and random selection — the assumption that Nurse A was innocent — is reasonable or not in the light of the data.

The logical structure of all statistical tests is as follows. The investigator sets out with all necessary assumptions, including the null hypothesis, built into the model. All but the null hypothesis are considered to constitute a reasonable description of how the data were generated; the null hypothesis is considered to be only a *possible* feature of this description. A calculation is then performed, using all the assumptions, in order to determine the probability of the results falling within a specified range — in the case of Jung's data, the probability of 19 or more out of 34 selected balls being red, or 19 or more out of 34 imperfect reproductions being associated with critical words. If this event is found to be unlikely, that is if its probability turns out to be small, then the investigator concludes that the null hypothesis is false and it is rejected. A numerical value, called a *significance level,* is given. The significance level shows how improbable it is, assuming the null hypothesis to be true, for the data to fall within the specified range. The more unlikely it is, the more confidence we may place in the *alternative hypothesis.* In the case of Jung's data, the alternative hypothesis is that the balls were not selected blindly or at random, in other words that Nurse A was guilty.

It is clear that the whole thrust of statistical analysis of this type is directed at calculating probabilities. Before proceeding with the analysis of Jung's data, it is therefore necessary to clarify the concept of probability and to explain some basic rules for making the appropriate calculations.

Probability

The probability of a head in a single toss of an unbiased coin is one in two or $\frac{1}{2}$. The probability of a six in a single toss of an unbiased die is $\frac{1}{6}$. In any such *random experiment*, to use the usual terminology of statistics, the set of all possible outcomes is called the *sample space*. The sample space of the coin-tossing random experiment contains two elements which we may label H and T, and the sample space of the die-tossing random experiment contains the six elements 1, 2, 3, 4, 5, and 6. The first basic rule for calculating probabilities is illustrated by these two simple examples. Most people have discovered this rule from playing games of chance. It may be stated formally as follows. If the N possible outcomes or *elementary events* in the sample space of a random experiment are all equally probable, then the probability of any one of them is $\frac{1}{N}$.

We must now consider a slightly more complicated problem. Statistical calculations often centre on the probabilities of *compound events* which are composed of sets of elementary events. If a random experiment consists of tossing a coin twice, for example, what is the probability of exactly one head coming up? The event is compound because two elements belong to the set, namely head on first toss only and head on second toss only. People often find this kind of problem confusing. They know what the probability is of a head on the first toss and a head on the second toss, but are not sure how to use this knowledge to calculate the probability of a head on *either* the first *or* the second toss. Actually, the problem can be handled in essentially the same way as one involving an elementary event. We simply list the equally probable elementary events of the sample space and count. In this case, the sample space contains four equally probable elementary events, *HH, HT, TH, TT*. Two of these belong to the set we are interested in, namely the set of elementary events containing exactly one head. The probability of the compound event, exactly one head in two tosses, is therefore $\frac{2}{4}$ or $\frac{1}{2}$.

What, then, is the probability that a single ball selected at random from an urn containing 37 red and 63 black balls will be red? The answer is $\frac{37}{100}$ because there are 100 equally probable elementary events in the sample space (100 equally probable outcomes of the random experiment) and 37 of them belong to the specified set. We are now ready to state the fundamental rule for calculating probabilities. If the sample space consists of equally probable elementary events, then the probability P of any event A (elementary or compound) is given by Formula 1.

$$P(A) = \frac{\text{number of elementary events in } A}{\text{number of equally probable elementary events}} \quad (1)$$

We come now to the *multiplication rule* for *joint events*. If the probability of a head in one toss of a coin is $\frac{1}{2}$, and the probability of a head in a second toss is also $\frac{1}{2}$, then what is the probability of the joint event of heads on both tosses? By listing the elementary events in this random experiment and counting, we can find the answer. Of the four equally probable elementary events, *HH, HT, TH, TT,* only one contains heads on both tosses. According to Formula 1, the probability of the joint event is therefore $\frac{1}{4}$. This method is rather cumbersome in more complicated cases. What, for example, is the probability of two sixes in two tosses of die? By listing the elementary events and applying Formula 1, the answer could be found: it is $\frac{1}{36}$.

From these two examples, the reader may have guessed the multiplication rule for joint events. The probability of two heads in two tosses of a coin is $(\frac{1}{2})(\frac{1}{2}) = \frac{1}{4}$, and the probability of two sixes in two tosses of a die is $(\frac{1}{6})(\frac{1}{6}) = \frac{1}{36}$. The multiplication rule may be generalized for more than two events and stated formally as follows. If the probability of Event A is p_1, the probability of Event B is p_2, ... , and the probability of Event K is p_n, and if these events are *stochastically independent*, then their joint probability is given by Formula 2.

$$P(A \text{ and } B \dots \text{ and } K) = p_1 p_2 p_n \quad (2)$$

There is no cause to be alarmed by the ugly phrase *stochastically independent*. In everyday language, this means simply that knowing whether or not one event has occurred tells us nothing about the likelihood of the other. Successive tosses of a coin or a die are stochastically independent in this sense, since knowing what has happened in the past would not affect our betting on a future outcome, provided of course that the coin or die is unbiased. Or, at least, it *should* not affect our betting: fortunes have been lost through gambling systems based on the *gambler's fallacy*, which is the belief that if a head has come up several times in a row the probability of a tail on the next toss is greater than ½.

If a random experiment consists of tossing a coin and a die simultaneously, then what is the probability of the event: head and six? The answer can be found from Formula 2, because the event: head, and the event: six, are obviously stochastically independent. The probability of the joint event: head and six, is therefore $(\frac{1}{2})(\frac{1}{6}) = \frac{1}{12}$. In two tosses of a coin, on the other hand, the probability of the joint event: head on first toss and two heads altogether, is not given by Formula 2. The individual probabilities are $\frac{1}{2}$ and $\frac{1}{4}$ (look at the sample space) but the joint probability is not $\frac{1}{8}$; it is obviously $\frac{1}{4}$. The multiplication rule does not work in this case because the individual events are not stochastically independent: knowing that a head came up on the first toss would increase our betting that heads would come up on both tosses.

The final rule for calculating probabilities is the *addition rule*. It applies to *mutually exclusive* events only. In tossing a coin twice, the event: two heads, and the event: at least one tail, are mutually exclusive because they cannot both occur; each event excludes the possibility of the other. What are their individual probabilities? The sample space contains the familiar four elements: *HH, HT, TH, TT*. The probability of two heads is evidently $\frac{1}{4}$, and the probability of at least one tail is $\frac{3}{4}$. Now what is the probability of the following event: *either* two heads *or* at least one tail? The answer can be found by counting the elementary events which belong to one or other of the sets; it is $\frac{4}{4}$. The reader may have noticed that this is also the sum of the probabilities of the individual events: $\frac{1}{4} + \frac{3}{4} = \frac{4}{4}$. The probability in this case is unity, which is another way of saying that the event is certain. It is important to notice that mutually exclusive events are not stochastically independent. Knowing whether or not one has occurred in the above example gives us certain knowledge of the other. This is why the probability of both events occurring is not the product of their individual probabilities; it is simply zero, which means that it is impossible.

The addition rule provides a useful method of calculating either/or probabilities for mutually exclusive events without resorting to counting the elementary events in the sample space. If the individual probabilities are known, then the probability of one or other of them occurring is simply the sum of their individual probabilities. The rule generalizes to two or more mutually exclusive events as follows. If Event A and Event B ... and Event K are all mutually exclusive, and if their respective probabilities are $p_1, p_2, \ldots p_n$, then

$$P(A \text{ or } B \ldots \text{ or } K) = p_1 + p_2 \cdots + p_n \tag{3}$$

Combinatorial Analysis

In theory, we could use the elementary rules of probability discussed above to solve many statistical problems, including the analysis of Jung's data. The sample space of Jung's investigation consists of all the ways of selecting 34 balls from an urn containing 37 red balls and 63 black balls, or of distributing 34 imperfect reproductions between 37 critical and 63 non-critical words. The probability we need to know is that of the compound event which is the set of selections containing 19 or more red balls or critical words. But to find the probabilities of the individual events we would have to list the sample space and resort to counting. Any attempt to approach the problem in this way is doomed to failure, because the list of elementary events would fill billions of stout volumes. The reader will therefore be delighted to learn that there are clever short-cut methods of counting by means of *combinatorial analysis*.

The first problem is to count the number of elements in the sample space. How many ways can 34 imperfect reproductions be distributed among 100 words? The best way of finding a general rule for solving this problem is by starting with a simpler version of it. Let us therefore ask instead: How many ways can three imperfect reproductions be distributed among five words? In terms of an equivalent simplified urn model, how many ways can three balls be selected from an urn containing five balls?

The first ball can be selected in any one of five different ways, since there are five balls to choose from. Having selected the first ball, there are four ways of selecting the second. To put it differently, for each of the five ways of selecting the first ball there are four ways of selecting the second. This means that there are 5 x 4 = 20 different ways of selecting the first two balls. This is equivalent to the number of ways of seating two people in five chairs: for each of the five chairs which may be chosen for the first person there remain four for the second, so two people can be seated in five chairs in 5 x 4 = 20 different ways. For each of the 20 ways of selecting the first two balls from an urn containing five balls, there remain three ways of selecting the third. There are thus 5 x 4 x 3 = 60 ways of selecting three balls from an urn containing five balls, and 60 ways of seating three people in five chairs. This is usually called the number of *permutations* of *r* things from among *N* things. The reader is invited to try, before reading on, to express the simple rule for permutations illustrated above in a general formula which works for any values of *N* and *r*; the need for a special system of notation will then be appreciated.

The rule is usually expressed with the use of factorial notation. In this notation, 2! (read 'two factorial') is equal to 2 x 1, 3! = 3 x 2 x 1, 4! = 4 x 3 x 2 x 1, and so on. For the rule to work when $N = r$ it is necessary to define 0! as being equal to 1. The general rule for permutations can then be written as shown in Formula 4.

$$\text{Number of permutations of } r \text{ things from among } N \text{ things} = \frac{N!}{(N-r)}. \qquad (4)$$

This formula simply expresses a general rule for the calculation used above. In the case we are considering, there are $N = 5$ balls in the urn and $r = 3$ of them are selected. The number of permutations or ways in which the selection can be made is therefore given by Formula 4 as shown below.

$$\frac{5!}{(5-3)!} = \frac{5 \times 4 \times 3 \times 2 \times 1}{2 \times 1} = \frac{120}{2} = 60.$$

Three balls can be selected from among five balls in 60 different ways; there are 60 permutations of three things from among five things.

An important feature of permutations is the fact that they take order into account. To understand this point, it is necessary to imagine that the balls in the urn are numbered from 1 to 5. Then one of the 60 permutations of three balls from among five consists of the balls numbered 1, 2 and 3, selected in that order. Another of the 60 permutations consists of the same three balls selected in the order 3, 2, 1, and a third consists of the ordered selection 2, 1, 3. In each case the same three balls are selected, but each selection is a different permutation because the order is different. In many kinds of problems, including the analysis of Jung's data, we need to count the number of ways of selecting r things from among N things *irrespective of order.* In these cases we do not distinguish between permutations like the three shown above; we are interested only in *which* balls are selected. The number of ways of selecting r things from among N things irrespective of the order of selection is called the number of *combinations* in order to distinguish it from the number of permutations. How can we calculate the number of combinations?

This problem can be solved fairly easily. For every combination there are a number of permutations, but how many? Suppose the balls are numbered 1, 2, 3, 4, and 5 as before. One combination consists of the first three balls. How many permutations are contained in this single combination? The answer is that there are six permutations containing the first three balls: 1 2 3, 1 3 2, 2 1 3, 2 3 1, 3 1 2, and 3 2 1. There are six permutations involving the same three balls because there are six ways of arranging three things in order. In general, it is obvious that there are as many permutations for any combination of *r* things as there are ways of arranging *r* things in order. This suggests a way of finding the number of combinations. We have a rule (Formula 4) for the number of permutations of *r* things from among *N* things. Each combination contains as many permutations as there are ways of arranging *r* things in order. So we can find the number of combinations by dividing the number of permutations by the number of ways of arranging *r* things in order.

But how many ways can *r* things be arranged in order? How many queues can *r* people form? We do not want to have to list the arrangements as we did with the three balls above and count them. We need a formula. In this case the formula could hardly be simpler. The number of arrangements of *r* things is clearly the number of ways of selecting *r* balls from a urn containing *N* balls, taking order into account, in the special case where $r = N$. We can arrange three things in order in as many ways as we can select three balls from an urn containing three balls, taking order into account. The answer is therefore given by Formula 4 when $r = N$; it is $r!/(r-r)! = r!/0! = r!/1 = r!$. The number of arrangements of *r* things is therefore $r!$.

We can now give a general rule for the number of combinations of *r* things from among *N* things. We have simply to divide the number of permutations given by Formula 4 by $r!$, which is the number of ways of arranging r things in order. The general formula for combinations is therefore

$$\text{Number of combinations of } r \text{ things from among } N \text{ things} = \frac{N!}{r!\,(N-r)!} = \binom{N}{r}. \quad \textbf{(5)}$$

Note that the symbol $\binom{N}{r}$ is not a conventional fraction: there is no horizontal line separating the N and the r. It is simply a shorthand way of writing $N!/r!\,(N-r)!$. It is known as the *binomial coefficient*.

We may apply the binomial coefficient to calculate the number of ways of selecting three balls from an urn containing five balls irrespective of the order of selection as follows:

$$\binom{5}{3} = \frac{5!}{3!(5-3)!} = \frac{5 \times 4 \times 3 \times 2 \times 1}{3 \times 2 \times 1 \times 2 \times 1} = 10.$$

An extremely useful device for finding binomial coefficients quickly is the remarkable number pattern known as *Pascal's triangle*. It is named after the seventeenth century French probabilist and philosopher, Blaise Pascal (1623-62), although historical research has shown that it was known to medieval Chinese and Indian mathematicians. The triangle begins with 1 at its apex, as shown in Table 5.

Rows								Diagonals
					0			
					1			
0				1		2		
1			1		1		3	
2		1		2		1		4
3		1	3		3		1	5
4	1		4	6		4	1	
5	1	5		10	10	5	1	

Table 5: *Pascal's triangle*

All other numbers in the triangle are simply the sums of the two numbers immediately above them. The 1's along the borders may be thought of as the sums of the 1's above them on one side and 0, or no number, on the other. The method of constructing the triangle is so simple that even a child can do it. The triangle can, of course, be extended downwards indefinitely.

Pascal's triangle is so rich in mathematical properties that many mathematicians consider it to be the most remarkable number pattern yet discovered. One of these properties provides a method of finding any binomial coefficient at a glance. The binomial coefficient $\binom{N}{r}$ is the number in the triangle where the Nth row and the rth diagonal intersect. To find the number of ways in which three balls can be selected from among five (irrespective of order), for example, simply look for the number in Pascal's triangle where Row 5 and Diagonal 3 intersect. The number located in this way is 10, which agrees with the result of calculation using the formula for the binomial coefficient $\binom{5}{3}$, as shown above. The mathematically-minded reader should not find it too difficult to prove why Pascal's triangle has this interesting property.

Returning to the sample space of Jung's investigation, the binomial coefficient may be used to find the number of ways in which 34 balls can be selected from an urn containing 100 balls, or the number of ways in which 34 imperfect reproductions can be distributed among 100 words. Since we do not wish to distinguish between different ordered sequences — only one order of selection is possible in a word-association test — this is equivalent to the number of combinations of 34 things from among 100 things. The answer must be $\binom{100}{34}$. This is an extremely large number, as anyone who tries to work it out will discover. It represents the number of elementary events in the sample space of Jung's investigation.

The next step is to calculate how many of these elementary events belong to the compound event we are interested in, namely the set of elementary events containing 19 or more imperfect reproductions to critical words. When we have answered this question we can calculate the *probability* of this compound event by simply applying Formula 1.

Hypergeometric Distribution

Consider once again the simplified urn model in which three balls are selected from among five. But imagine this time that three of the balls in the urn are red and two are black. Now let us choose a possible outcome of the random experiment: let us suppose that exactly two of the three selected balls turn out to be red. In how many ways can this selection be made (irrespective of order)?

This is most easily thought of as two separate but simultaneous selections. From the combinatorial methods discussed above, it is clear that two red balls can be selected from among the three red balls in the urn in $\binom{3}{2} = 3$ different ways. Similarly, one black ball can be selected from among the two black balls in $\binom{2}{1} = 2$ different ways. For each of the three ways of selecting the red balls there are two ways of selecting the black ball. The number of ways of selecting exactly two red balls *and* one black ball from this particular urn is therefore $\binom{3}{2}\binom{2}{1}$ or $(3)(2)$, which is 6.

We have already seen that the total number of ways of selecting three balls from among five is $\binom{5}{3}$, which is equal to 10. We now know that this selection can result in exactly two red balls and one black ball in 6 different ways. What, then is the *probability* that, of five balls selected, exactly two will be red and one black? If we can answer this question, then we will have come close to solving Jung's problem.

The reader who has grasped the elementary rules of probability will not find this problem very difficult. We know the number of equally probable events in the sample space: this is simply the number of ways of selecting three balls from among five, and it is equal to $\binom{5}{3}$. We also know the number of elementary events which belong to the set we are interested in, namely the number of ways of selecting the balls so that exactly two are red and one is black; this number is equal to $\binom{3}{2}\binom{2}{1}$. The desired probability is therefore given by

Formula 1; it is

$$\frac{\binom{3}{2}\binom{2}{1}}{\binom{5}{3}} = \frac{6}{10} = 0.6.$$

We have come a long way with our simplified version of Jung's problem. The next step is to express the method of calculation shown above in a general formula which can be applied to more difficult cases. To do this, we need a suitable set of symbols. Let the number of balls in the urn be represented by N, the number of red balls in the urn by R, the number of balls selected by r, and the number of red balls among those selected by x. We do not need a special symbol for the number of black balls in the urn, because this can be represented by $N - R$, nor do we need one for the number of black balls among those selected, since this is $r - x$. Using this notation, the general formula for finding exactly x red balls among r balls selected from an urn containing N balls of which R are red is shown in Formula 6.

$$P(x) = \frac{\binom{R}{x}\binom{N-r}{r-x}}{\binom{N}{r}}, \quad x = 0, 1, 2, \ldots \tag{6}$$

Formula 6 can be used to calculate the probability $P(x)$ of finding exactly x balls among those selected in any specific case. The calculation given above may be thought of as an application of this formula to find $P(2)$ when $N = 5$, $R = 3$, and $r = 3$; in that case $P(2)$ was found to be 0.6. Given any fixed N, R, and r, the formula may be used to calculate the probabilities $P(x)$ of *all possible* values of x or numbers of red balls among those selected. If this complete set of calculations is performed, the result is known as the *hypergeometric probability distribution*.

The concept of a probability distribution is one of the most important ideas in the theory of statistics, and it is worth dwelling on it for a moment. Strictly speaking, the following remarks apply in general to probability distributions of *discrete* random variables only. These distributions refer to random experiments in which the number of possible outcomes is finite or countable, as in the case we are considering in which $x = 0, 1, 2$, etc. With *continuous* random variables, the essential ideas are the same, but the mathematical machinery is somewhat different.

A probability distribution can be thought of as a list of mutually exclusive events covering the entire sample space of a random experiment, together with their respective probabilities. The events are not necessarily elementary, and they are not necessarily equally probable. In the simplified urn model, for example, each of the events whose probabilities are listed in the hypergeometric distribution is a compound event consisting of all the outcomes (elementary events) in which exactly x red balls are found among the r balls selected. One of the events in the hypergeometric distribution is represented by $x = 2$; it is the set of all possible selections of r balls containing exactly two red balls, and the corresponding probability of this compound event when $N = 5$, $R = 3$, and $r = 3$ is $P(2) = 0.6$, as shown in the calculation above. The complete hypergeometric distribution for these fixed values of N, R, and r is shown below.

Events:	x	0	1	2	3
Probabilities:	$P(x)$	0	0.3	0.6	0.1

This distribution gives the exact probabilities of finding exactly 0, 1, 2, or 3 red balls among the three selected. These events are mutually exclusive since it is impossible to find 0 *and* 1 or 1 *and* 3 red balls in a single selection, and so on. They represent an exhaustive partition of the sample space because there must be either 0, 1, 2, or 3 red balls in any given selection of three balls; one of these events is bound to occur. What is the probability of finding two *or more* red balls among those selected? This is equivalent to the probability of finding *either* two *or* three red balls. Since these events are mutually exclusive, the either/or addition rule given in Formula 3 is obviously applicable. The individual probabilities in question are 0.6 and 0.1 respectively; the probability of either two or three red balls is therefore 0.6 + 0.1 = 0.7. For the same reason, the complete set of values of $P(x)$ in a probability distribution must sum to unity: one of the events covered by the distribution is bound to occur.

Thus $0 + 0.3 + 0.6 + 0.1 = 1.0$.

The hypergeometric is only one of a large number of probability distributions known to statisticians. The type of distribution used for a particular statistical calculation obviously depends upon the nature of the random experiment implied by the model. For random experiments which can be formulated in terms of the urn model used for Jung's data, the appropriate probability distribution is evidently the hypergeometric distribution defined by Formula 6. This distribution gives the probabilities of all possible outcomes of such experiments.

Let us interrupt our analysis of Jung's data once again in order to apply the hypergeometric distribution to solve the problem raised in the *Johnson v. Louisiana* case mentioned earlier. The problem in that case was one of calculating the probability that five jurors, selected at random from among a 12-member jury containing nine who voted to convict and three who voted to acquit, would all have voted to convict. This can obviously be modelled in terms of a random selection of five balls from an urn containing nine red and three black balls. The probability that all five of the selected balls will be red is found by substituting in the hypergeometric formula with $N = 12$, $R = 9$, $r = 5$, and $x = 5$:

$$P(5) = \frac{\binom{9}{5}\binom{3}{0}}{\binom{12}{5}} = \frac{(126)(1)}{792} = 0.159.$$

The probability of this event is less than 16 in 100. We can therefore conclude that a random selection of five people from among the jurors who convicted Johnson would produce a five-member jury which in more than 84 per cent of cases would have insufficient votes to convict unanimously.

Fisher's Exact Probability Test

In order to solve Jung's problem, and in most other statistical calculations as well, we need to find the probability, not of a single event in the distribution, but of a range of events. In this case we want to know the probability, not of *exactly* 19 red balls among those selected, but of 19 *or more*. The way in which a probability distribution can be used to find the probability of a range of events has been illustrated above. The statistical analysis carried out in this way by adding together a range of probabilities of the hypergeometric distribution is called *Fisher's exact probability test*, although it was in fact developed independently and simultaneously by Fisher, Irwin, and Yates in 1934-5.

We are ready at long last to calculate the probability of the range of events we are concerned with in Jung's investigation. The required probability is that of finding 19 or more red balls among 34 selected at random from an urn containing 100 balls of which 37 are red. We therefore set $N = 100$, $R = 37$, and $r = 34$ and calculates the values of $P(x)$ for $x = 19$, $x = 20$, ..., $x = 34$, using the version of the hypergeometric formula shown below.

$$P(x) = \frac{\binom{37}{x} \binom{100-34}{34-x}}{\binom{100}{34}}, \quad x = 19, 20, \dots 34.$$

The required probability is then given by summing all the resulting values of $P(x)$.

Unfortunately, the computation required for using Fisher's exact probability test in cases like this where the numbers are large is extremely cumbersome. There are, however, several short methods of computation which give very close approximations to the exact hypergeometric probabilities with large samples of data. To cut a long story short and to finally reach a verdict on Nurse A, the probability turns out to be slightly less than 0.01, or as it is normally expressed by statisticians, we can reject the null hypothesis at a significance level of $p < 0.01$.

The null hypothesis can be rejected with considerable confidence. This does not mean that the probability of Nurse A's innocence is less than 0.01 and the probability that she was guilty is therefore more than 0.99. It means that *if she was innocent,* and if the model used was a reasonable one, then a pattern of responses as seemingly incriminating as hers is improbable: its probability is less than 0.01. Although such an unlikely event *may* have happened, it is much more reasonable to reject the null hypothesis and accept the alternative hypothesis that Nurse A was guilty, and we can make this judgment with more conviction than Jung was entitled to.

A Word About the t Test

The reader who has followed each step in the analysis of Jung's data already understands the essential ideas behind statistical hypothesis testing. All statistical tests are based upon the same fundamental principles, although of course the particular models used, and the corresponding probability distributions on which the tests are based, vary from one case to the next. At the beginning of this chapter, for example, an imaginary set of data showing the scores of two groups of children on a foreign language test after receiving different methods of instruction were given. A chain of argument, no different in principle from that used for analysing Jung's data, could be used to find the probability of a difference between the two groups as large or larger than the difference given in the imaginary data. By constructing a suitable model, a probability distribution could be found for testing the null hypothesis that there was no difference between the effectiveness of the two teaching methods, in other words that the differences in the scores were due entirely to chance.

A convenient statistical test in this case turns out to be the *t* test which is based upon probabilities of the *t* distribution. The *t* distribution, like the hypergeometric distribution, gives probabilities for all possible ranges of events in certain kinds of random experiments, although of course the form of the *t* distribution is quite different from that of the hypergeometric. The *t* test was used to calculate the probability which was mentioned at the beginning of the chapter in connection with the imaginary data. The calculation showed that the probability of a difference between the two groups of scores as large or larger than the difference shown was rather high; it was found to be in the region of 0.25. The null hypothesis could not therefore be rejected with confidence. The mathematical basis of the t distribution is too difficult to be explained here. But it is desirable to present the reader with the logic of a distribution quite different from the hypergeometric in order to place the latter in perspective. Let us therefore turn to a distribution which will enable us to calculate the probabilities of bombs falling on London and deaths from horse kicks in the Prussian Army referred to earlier.

Binomial Distribution

In the urn model which was used as a basis for analysing Jung's data, an implicit assumption was that the balls were selected *without replacement*. For some statistical analyses, a model in which sampling is carried out *with replacement* is more appropriate.

Consider the following model. An urn contains 100 balls of which 37 are red and 63 are black as before. Now suppose a ball is selected at random, its colour is noted, and it is then *replaced* in the urn. Assuming that five random selections are made, the ball being replaced after each selection, what is the probability that exactly three of the five selected balls will be red?

Many seemingly unrelated sets of data may be modelled in this way. The model is appropriate if the following three features are present in the data: each single observation belongs to one of two categories, usually labelled S (for *success*) and F (for *failure*); the outcomes are stochastically independent in so far as one observation would not affect our betting on another; and the probability of success on each observation is the same.

In terms of the revised urn model, the selection of a red ball may be labelled S and the selection of a black ball F. Since the selections are made at random, the condition of stochastic independence is satisfied. The probability of success on each observation is clearly $\frac{37}{100}$; this follows directly from Formula 1.

Data of this kind are called *independent Bernoulli trials* after the seventeenth century Swiss probabilist, James Bernoulli, who first analysed them. It is convenient when discussing Bernoulli trials to label the probability of success p and the probability of failure q. In the example we are considering, $p = \frac{37}{100}$ and $q = \frac{63}{100}$. In the urn model used to show how Jung's data were generated, it was assumed that a fixed number of balls were selected all at once, or what amounts to the same thing, that the balls were selected one after the other *without* being replaced in the urn. This implies that the values of p and q changed after each ball was selected. The probability of the first ball being red is $\frac{37}{100}$, but the probability of the second ball being red depends upon the outcome of the first selection; if the first ball was red, then the probability on the second trial is $\frac{36}{99}$, otherwise it is $\frac{37}{99}$. In Jung's investigation, the value of p (and the value of q) is not the same from trial to trial, and the imperfect and perfect reproductions of Nurse A were therefore not modelled by a series of independent Bernoulli trials. The revised urn model differs from the one used to generate the hypergeometric distribution in the single way that p and q are always the same — they are *stationary* — and this enables rather elegant calculations to be made.

Let us begin with one possible outcome of the random experiment of selecting five balls from the urn with replacement. What is the probability of the following particular sequence of successes and failures (red and black balls): *SSFFS*?

This question can be answered rather easily. The probability that the first ball is red is p, which in this case is $\frac{37}{100}$. The probability that the second ball is red is also p. The probabilities that the third and fourth balls are black are each q, or $\frac{63}{100}$. Finally, the probability that the last ball is red is p. Since these five events are stochastically independent, we can use Formula 2 to find the probability of the joint event *SSFFS*; all we have to do is to multiply the five individual probabilities together. The probability of the sequence *SSFFS* is therefore $ppqqp$, or simply p^3q^2. In this case it works out as $\left(\frac{37}{100}\right)^3 \left(\frac{63}{100}\right)^2 = 0.02$.

What is the general rule? Can we give a compact formula to find the probability of any particular sequence containing a certain number of successes in a certain number of Bernoulli trials? By simply generalizing the calculation given above, and letting r stand for the number of successes and N for the number of trials, we may express the rule as follows: $p^r q^{N-r}$. It is important to note that this expression gives the probability of a particular ordered sequence or permutation of successes and failures. But the probability of each different permutation containing the same *number* of successes and failures is the same. The probability of the sequence *SSSFF* is also $p^3 q^2 = 0.02$, and so is the sequence *FSSSF*.

In many statistical problems, we wish to know the probability of finding a particular number of red balls among those selected — a particular number of S's — rather than that of any specific ordered sequence of S's and F's. In our revised urn model, what is the probability that exactly three of the five selected balls will be red? This event obviously consists of all the particular sequences of three S's and two F's. We know what each of their individual probabilities are: they are $p^3 q^2$ in each case. We also know that the particular sequences are mutually exclusive events. Formula 3, which gives the addition rule for mutually exclusive events, therefore applies. To find the probability that exactly

three of the five selected balls will be red, we need to add together the probabilities of the individual sequences; this gives the probability of one or another of these sequences of three S's and two F's occurring, which is the probability we are after. In other words, we need to add $p^3q^2 + p^3q^2 + \ldots$ as many times as there are different sequences of three S's and two F's, or equivalently, to multiply p^3q^2 by the number of possible sequences.

But how many different sequences of three S's and two F's are there? A moment's reflection shows that this is logically equivalent to asking how many ways three things can be selected from among five things. If five black balls are arranged in order, the number of ways of selecting three of them to paint red is clearly the same as the number of sequences of three red and two black balls, or of three S's and two F's. As shown earlier, the number of ways of selecting three things from among five things is given by the binomial coefficient $\binom{5}{3}$, which works out as $\frac{5!}{3!(5-3)!} = 10$. Letting N stand for the number of Bernoulli trials and r for the number of successes, the general expression for the number of particular sequences containing exactly r successes and $N - r$ failures is $\binom{N}{r}$.

We are now ready to calculate the *probability* of a specified number of successes *(r)* in a fixed number of Bernoulli trials *(N)*, for example three red balls among the five selected from the urn in our revised model. We have established that each *particular sequence* of r successes (and $N - r$ failures) has the probability p^rq^{N-r}. We have also established that there are $\binom{N}{r}$ such sequences. To find the desired probability, we need only to multiply the individual probability of each particular sequence by $\binom{N}{r}$, the number of mutually exclusive sequences. The probability of exactly r successes in N independent Bernoulli trials with probability of success p and probability of failure q is therefore given by Formula 7.

$$P(r) = \binom{N}{r} p^rq^{N-r}, \quad r = 0, 1, 2, \ldots N. \tag{7}$$

Given any fixed N and p (q is always $1 - p$), we may use Formula 8 to calculate $P(r)$ for *all possible* values of r, or numbers of red balls among those selected. The resulting set of probabilities $P(r)$ and corresponding events r is known as the *binomial probability distribution*. One of the events represented by the binomial distribution when $N = 5$ and $p = \frac{37}{100}$ is, for example, exactly three red balls among those selected. The corresponding probability $P(3)$ can be found by substituting in Formula 7 with $r = 3$. The probability of this event is

$$P(3) = \binom{5}{3} \left(\frac{37}{100}\right)^3 \left(\frac{63}{100}\right)^2, = 0.20.$$

The binomial distribution is different in form from the hypergeometric distribution discussed earlier. It can be viewed as a list of mutually exclusive events covering the sample space of a random experiment of a different kind from that given by the hypergeometric distribution, together with a different set of probabilities for the events. The probabilities of the complete set of events given in the distribution sum to unity as before, since the events are mutually exclusive and exhaustive, and the probabilities of any selected range of events may be added to find the probability of one or another of them occurring. An analysis of data using this procedure is called the *binomial test*; it has often been used for analysing the results of psychological investigations of certain kinds.

We return now to the bombing of London mentioned earlier in this chapter. It will be remembered that 537 bombs fell on an area divided into 576 sectors of equal size. We wish to discover whether, as most Londoners believed, the bombs tended to fall in a non-random pattern. The correct method of analysis is to state the null hypothesis that the bombs fell purely at random, to calculate the expected distribution of hits on this assumption, and to compare these results with the observed distribution of hits.

Assuming the null hypothesis, and a few other features of how the data were generated which seem reasonable, the number of bombs falling on a *single* sector may be modelled as a series of independent Bernoulli trials. In this case, the urn contains 576 balls, of which 1 is red. Each trial corresponds to the falling of a bomb; if a red ball is selected (a success), the particular sector in question is hit, while if a black ball is selected (a failure), the bomb falls on one of the other 575 sectors. The probability of success p on each trial is $\frac{1}{576}$, and the probability of failure q is $\frac{575}{576}$. The number of independent Bernoulli trials N is the number of bombs which fell, 537.

The next step is to calculate the entire binomial distribution for $N = 537$ and $p = \frac{1}{576}$. This is done by substituting these figures in Formula 8 together with $r = 0$, $r = 1$, $r = 2$, and so on. For example, when $r = 2$, the corresponding value of $P(2)$ gives the probability of a single sector being hit exactly twice. The probability is

$$P(2) = \binom{537}{2}\left(\tfrac{1}{576}\right)^2 \left(\tfrac{575}{576}\right)^{535}.$$

The direct computation of this probability is obviously very cumbersome, but once again there are short methods which give extremely close approximations to the exact binomial probabilities. The above probability works out at approximately $P(2) = 0.172$. If the null hypothesis is true, that is if the bombs fell at random, then the probability that any single sector would be hit exactly twice is thus 0.172. Since there were 576 sectors in all, the expected number of sectors which would be hit exactly twice is therefore $0.172 \times 576 = 99$. The number of sectors which are expected to be hit exactly twice on the basis of chance alone is accordingly given in Table 3 above as 99. This table also gives the expected number of sectors corresponding to 0, 1, 3, 4, 5 + hits, which were all calculated in exactly the same way. The extremely close fit between the expected and observed distributions in the table indicates that the bombs did, in fact, fall at random over South London.

The method of calculating the expected distribution of 122 deaths due to horse kicks among 200 Prussian Army Corps is essentially the same. In this case the urn contains 200 balls, of which one is red. The probability of a death due to horse kicks occurring in a single specified corps corresponds to that of selecting the red ball from the urn; it is $p = \frac{1}{200}$ if the null hypothesis is true, ie if the accidents struck at random. The number of independent Bernoulli trials in this case is 122, since this is the total number of deaths from horse kicks which occurred. The expected distribution of deaths shown in Table 4 may be found by multiplying each of the appropriate binomial probabilities $P(0)$, $P(1)$, $P(2)$, $P(3)$, and $P(4)$ by 200, the number of corps. Once again, the observed and expected distributions agree extremely well, indicating that the accidents were in fact distributed randomly.

From a purely intuitive point of view, the 'even' distribution of exactly one death in each of 122 of the 200 corps seems fairly likely; in fact many people believe this to be the most likely distribution. The probability of this event may be calculated as follows. The probability that the first accident will strike in a corps which has not previously suffered a death from horse kicks is $\frac{200}{200}$, that is, it is certain. When the second accident strikes, assuming that it strikes at random, it is equally likely to occur in any one of the 200 corps. At this point, 199 of the corps have not previously experienced such an accident. The probability that it will occur in one of these 199 corps is $\frac{199}{200}$. The probability that the third death will occur in a previously unaffected corps is $\frac{198}{200}$. If the process continues in this way, the probability of the final (122nd) accident occurring in a corps which has not previously suffered any deaths from horse kicks is $\frac{79}{200}$. If the null hypothesis is true, that is to say if the distribution of accidents is random, then these events are stochastically independent. According to Formula 2, therefore, the probability of the joint event: exactly one death from horse kicks in each of 122 of the 200 corps, is

$$\left(\tfrac{200}{200}\right)\left(\tfrac{199}{200}\right)\left(\tfrac{198}{200}\right) \cdots \left(\tfrac{79}{200}\right) = 1.321 \times 10^{-21}.$$

This number is roughly equal to one in ten thousand million million million.

Concluding Comments

The results of psychological investigations are seldom completely clear-cut. It is not always obvious what conclusions are justified by them. Sometimes the

137

conclusions which seem obvious are in fact wrong. The reader's faith in intuitive or 'commonsense' interpretations of data may have been seriously shaken by some of the examples given in this chapter. Similar problems of interpreting results arise in numerous other areas of investigation, including agriculture, nuclear physics, sociology, and medical research. Ever since the 1930s it has been customary to analyse the results of investigations in such fields with the techniques of inferential statistics. The application of these techniques is often quite straightforward, and requires little mathematical expertise. An understanding of the ideas behind them poses more of a challenge.

Unfortunately, many students of psychology (and many of their teachers) are content to treat statistics simply as a set of mechanical skills, which probably explains why statistics is seldom a popular part of undergraduate psychology syllabuses. There is nothing particularly interesting in applying standard formulas to standard types of data or in learning and remembering which are the 'correct' formulas for which types of data. And there is something deeply unsatisfying, particularly to someone with a questioning mind, in reporting the results of statistical tests, or in having to accept the probability levels published in technical research reports, without any real understanding of what they mean or where they come from. It is one thing to 'know' that a null hypothesis ought to be rejected because the probability given by the statistical test is smaller than some specified significance level, but quite another to understand what this really means and how the statistical test leads to such a conclusion. I have therefore attempted here to explain the underlying theory of statistical tests in plain language which anyone with a modicum of school algebra can understand. Some of the ideas are subtle and may require reflection; but anyone who has read slowly and carefully should have been rewarded with a fairly sound understanding of the fundamental principles of inferential statistics and why it is used in psychology, and will also no doubt appreciate the fact that statistics is an attractive and interesting subject in its own right.

Further Reading

A quite outstanding introduction to the theory of probability, which takes the reader from elementary ideas to an extremely advanced level, is Feller, W. *An Introduction to Probability Theory and Its Applications*, 3rd ed., Vol. I (New York: Wiley, 1968). There are many good and bad books devoted to applications of statistics in psychology and related fields. One which strikes a nice balance between theory and technique is Hays, W.L. *Statistics for the Social Sciences*, 2nd ed. (New York: Holt, Rinehart and Winston, 1973). A classic text concerned with statistical tests of a special kind, and including a discussion of Fisher's exact probability test, is Siegel, S. *Nonparametric Statistics for the Behavioral Sciences* (New York: McGraw-Hill, 1956). Jung's investigation, which provided the raw data for the main statistical analysis in this chapter, was reported in a paper entitled 'The Association Method' (*The American Journal of Psychology*, 1910, **21**, 219-69).

5. The Origins and Development of Psychology

History helps us to understand the present. To those who have no knowledge of the history of psychology, the areas of research outlined in Chapter 3 may seem to be a rather whimsical collection of topics; they make more sense when they are viewed in their proper historical context. Before examining the various branches of contemporary psychology, it is therefore illuminating to investigate its roots.

Important advances in psychological knowledge were made as long ago as the sixth century BC. But it was not until the late nineteenth century that psychology emerged as an independent discipline in its own right. Until then, the study of the mind and behaviour was always treated as a branch of philosophy. During the eighteenth and nineteenth centuries, developments in biology began to suggest novel approaches to problems of mental philosophy, and towards the end of this period psychology finally reached maturity and gained its independence. As Hermann Ebbinghaus, one of the pioneers of the new discipline, remarked in 1907, 'psychology has a long past but a short history'. A glimpse into its philosophical and biological past will make its passage to its short history easier to understand.

Philosophical Roots

Psychology perhaps has its origins in the thinking of the school of Ancient Greek philosophers of the sixth and fifth centuries BC, who are known as the pre-Socratics. They were the first to realize that the brain plays a part in all mental experience. More specifically, they realized that the eyes and the ears cannot see and hear on their own without the help of the brain. In addition to this, they gave serious attention to the fact that people differ not only in physical appearance but also in temperament, or what psychologists later came to call personality. According to the pre-Socratics, the temperamental differences between people result from the mixture of humours in their bodies (blood, phlegm, melancholy or black bile, and choler or yellow bile), just as the properties of substances derive from the mixture of elements of which they are composed (earth, air, fire, and water).

Looking back on pre-Socratic philosophy, what seems most striking to us is the absence of any concept of the soul; though Anaxagorus, for instance, held that mind causes all movement and is distinct from the substance it moves, he believed not in individual minds or souls but in a generalized mind throughout the universe. It was only towards the end of the fifth century BC that the concept of the individual soul became current. A short while later, Aristotle (384-22 BC) raised it to a position of great importance in *De Anima*, in effect the first and most influential textbook of psychology; he held that mind is not outside but *inside* matter, and that mind cannot exist without matter. The doctrine of the soul dominated European thinking throughout the medieval period, but the religious dogma that man is completely subject to the inexorable will of God obviously inhibited any possible objective study of the relationship between mind and matter. Philosophers of the Renaissance, though subject to less rigorous religious restraints, were more interested in the use and potential of the mind than in its nature.

René Descartes, the seventeenth century French thinker, was the first major philosopher of the post-medieval period, and is often called the father of modern philosophy. His importance in the history of psychology arises from his theory about the relationship between the mind and the body. Descartes was the first philosopher to distinguish clearly between mental experiences, such as thoughts, feelings, and perceptions on the one hand, and physical events, such as bodily functions and behaviour on the other. A human body, according to Descartes, is simply a machine which obeys ordinary physical laws. Mental experiences, for their part, are the work of the soul. The soul is immaterial, that is to say it does not occupy space like a physical object, and it is also free from the restrictions of physical laws. Philosophers who wish to be unkind to Descartes have labelled his theory 'the ghost in the machine'.

Many philosophers before Descartes had grappled with the problem: Where do mental experiences take place? The pre-Socratics opted for the brain. The later Greek philosopher Plato (427-347 BC), located desire in the liver, courage in the heart, and reason in the brain. Plato's pupil, Aristotle, strayed even further from the mark: he chose the heart as the seat of all mental experiences. For Descartes, mental experiences are functions of the soul which, since it is immaterial, cannot be located in any particular part of the body. But it seemed obvious to Descartes that the soul and the body somehow manage to influence each other, and that this interaction must take place somewhere in the body. A desire to write (a mental experience) can cause the hand to move (a physical event) and, conversely, an injury to the foot (a physical event) can cause an experience of pain (a mental experience).

Descartes knew that the information received by the sense organs is transmitted to the brain. He therefore narrowed his search for the organ of interaction between soul and body to the brain. He eventually identified a part of the brain known as the pineal gland (actually one of the endocrine glands) as the seat of soul-body interaction. The pineal gland seemed an obvious choice for three reasons. First, it is located in the very centre of the brain. Second, only human beings were thought to possess souls, and Descartes (wrongly) believed that only they were blessed with pineal glands; he was not well-versed in comparative anatomy. Third and most important, the pineal gland is the only part of the main structure of the brain which is not duplicated in two halves. When the images from the two eyes are perceived by the soul, they are fused together into a single picture. The pineal gland seemed to Descartes to be the only part of the brain capable of performing this marvellous feat of integration; if the soul-body interaction took place anywhere else in the brain, we would all suffer from permanent double vision. For all these reasons, the pineal gland seemed to be the natural choice. According to Descartes, the soul influences the body and the body influences the soul quite simply through the action of the pineal gland in causing 'vital spirits' to flow through the body in various directions.

Descartes' theory did not seem, to later generations of philosophers or indeed some of Descartes' contemporaries, to be a satisfactory solution to the problem posed by the fact that mental experiences and physical events seem to belong to two quite separate realms. A mental experience like grief may be accompanied by a bodily process like weeping; but grief is not the same thing as weeping, it is an altogether different kind of thing from *any* purely physical process. If mental experiences and physical events are entirely different kinds of things, how can they influence each other as they seem to do? How can a mental (non-physical) cause have a physical effect and vice versa? To put it crudely, how can a thought move a muscle? This is the famous *mind-body problem* which has occupied philosophers ever since the time of Descartes. The various solutions to the mind-body problem which have been suggested since the seventeenth century have been integral to the development of psychology.

Descartes accepted the commonsense idea that the mind and the body do indeed influence each other, rejecting the theory of his English contemporary Thomas Hobbes who held that all that exists is matter and that all thoughts and ideas are in fact merely a form of motion taking place in the nerves and the brain. The approach of Descartes and his followers to the mind-body problem is known as *interactionism*. But Descartes' pineal gland theory does not really solve the problem at all. In fact, he does not seem even to have realized that such a problem existed until it was pointed out to him. The story of the discovery of the problem is worth telling.

In 1643, Princess Elizabeth, the daughter of King James I of England, wrote a letter to Descartes. She had read Descartes' recently published *Meditations on First Philosophy* and had noticed the mind-body problem immediately. She stated the problem simply and clearly, and requested an answer from Descartes. In his reply, Descartes acknowledged that he had not fully dealt with the problem, and offered an incomprehensible explanation in terms of ideas about gravity. Princess Elizabeth immediately penned a second letter. 'I cannot understand', she wrote, 'the way that the soul, unextended and immaterial, moves the body, in terms of the idea you used to have about gravity ... or why the soul is so much governed by the body, when it ... has nothing in common with it'. Descartes' second reply was no more helpful than his first. The soul-body interaction, he said, can be understood 'only in an obscure way' through intellect and imagination. But 'those who never do philosophise ... have no doubt that the soul moves the body and the body acts on the soul'. He expressed his 'sincere admiration' for her Highness's intelligence, and admitted that his explanation in terms of gravity had been 'lame'. He concluded his letter by warning her that, although it was a good thing to study the principles of philosophy, 'it would be very harmful to occupy one's intellect often with meditating on them'. The exchange of letters between Princess Elizabeth and Descartes suggests that the credit for realizing the mind-body problem should go to the princess rather than to the 'father of modern philosophy'.

The century which followed Descartes is often called the Age of Reason. It was a century in which a critical and rational approach to understanding flourished. The character of eighteenth century philosophy is partly explained by the dazzling successes which had recently been achieved in the physical sciences by Galileo, Kepler, and, above all, Newton (1642-1727). But the 1700s were lean times in the history of psychology. In order to understand why natural philosophy (what is now called physical science) thrived at the expense of mental philosophy during the eighteenth century, it is necessary to reflect for a moment on the impact of Newton's theory of mechanics.

Newton's theory, which came to light towards the end of the seventeenth century, is probably the boldest and most successful theory in the entire history of science. On the basis of four almost childishly simple postulates, Newton was able to explain not only apples falling on people's heads, but also the ebb and flow of tides, and the peculiar motions of all the known planets, moons, and comets in the solar system. The motions of the celestial bodies could be predicted from the theory with an astonishing degree of accuracy. (In 1859, it was discovered that Mercury drifts from the predicted orbit by a tiny angle of 43 seconds of arc, or approximately one hundredth of a degree, *per century*, which shows that Newton's theory is indeed oversimplified. Einstein's improved theory does not suffer from this imperfection).

The impression created by the almost miraculous success of Newtonian mechanics was that before long natural science would be able to explain everything. A complete understanding of the world, in terms of matter in motion, seemed to many to be within easy grasp. The existing body of scientific knowledge was so powerful that all that was needed, so it seemed, was to fill in the missing details. The principles of mechanics were examined for answers to all remaining questions about nature.

In France, where Descartes' influence had been strongest, the search began for a solution to the mind-body problem more in keeping with the spirit of the times. The *philosophes* of the Enlightenment, the period leading up to the French Revolution of 1789, began to lean towards materialism. French thinkers were fully aware of the achievements of Newton across the English Channel, partly through the writings of Voltaire, who spent a period of exile in England. A new solution to the mind-body problem with a strongly physical bias became fashionable in France. The new idea was expressed in an extreme form by La Mettrie, who published a book in 1748 entitled *L'Homme Machine* or, freely translated, *The Human Machine*.

None of the French materialists, not even La Mettrie, were thoroughgoing in their materialism. None went as far as suggesting that mental experiences do not exist at all. They adopted a diluted version of materialism which came to be called *epiphenomenalism*. According to this doctrine, mental experiences are real, but they are merely trivial by-products (epiphenomena) of one special class of physical events, namely brain processes. Physical events can cause mental experiences, but mental experiences, which are mere epiphenomena, cannot cause physical events: the mind is to the body as a shadow is to a moving object. The epiphenomenalist theory allows a one-way interaction between body and mind, rather than the two-way interactionism suggested by Descartes (and by common sense). It acknowledges that an injury to the foot can, in a purely mechanical way, produce a mental experience of pain; but it denies that a thought can move a muscle.

The doctrine of epiphenomenalism acted on the burning issues of mental philosophy like a steady drizzle. It led people to regard mental experiences as unimportant and uninteresting. Since they were considered to be mere epiphenomena which could not have any effects of their own, mental experiences seemed hardly worth investigating. And if they were to be investigated, the only way of doing so seemed to be by studying the machinery of the body, particularly the brain. These prejudices gained a firm foothold during the period of the eighteenth century Enlightenment, and they help to explain why the study of mental processes is a fairly recent development. It was only after the epiphenomenalist solution to the mind-body problem went into decline that psychology emerged as an active and independent field of research.

French materialism was largely responsible for the popularity of epiphenomenalism and the resulting neglect of psychological questions during the eighteenth century. But it also had positive effects on related areas of research which were to be helpful in an indirect way to the later development of psychology. To begin with, biological research, particularly in the area of human physiology, was enormously stimulated by materialist ideas. Many crucial discoveries were made about the sense organs, the nervous system, and the brain, especially in France and England. There were also certain developments in the field of medicine, which were later to have important repercussions on psychology. During the 1770s, the French physician Franz Anton Mesmer introduced the scientific community to his work on 'animal magnetism'. Mesmer was without doubt a quack, but the trances which he induced in his patients raised interesting questions. Mesmerism formed the basis of later more reputable research on hypnosis. Finally, an entirely new way of looking at madness evolved. Since medieval times, madness had been regarded as the result of spirit possession, and its unfortunate victims were either executed or subjected to imprisonment and various forms of torture designed to exorcize the evil spirits. Materialist thinking led to a reinterpretation of madness as a kind of illness, caused by physical disorders of the brain, which required medical rather than spiritual forms of treatment. This new theory of madness led Philippe Pinel to unchain the insane and liberate them from the dungeons of the Paris mad-houses, and executions for witchcraft came to an end throughout Europe.

From the early nineteenth century onwards, the doctrine of epiphenomenalism gradually lost its appeal. Its decline is largely attributable to its inability to assimilate the facts of mental life which came to light during this period. Brain research was hopelessly unsuccessful in explaining mental experiences, mesmerism turned out to have no physical basis, and mental illnesses were discovered which were not caused by physical disorders of the brain or nervous system.

One of the most dismal failures in the history of brain research was the movement known as *phrenology* which flourished in the early decades of the nineteenth century. Its founder, Franz Joseph Gall, was an anatomist who believed that mental faculties are located in specific parts of the brain. The most highly developed faculties were supposed to be visible by enlargements of the brain (and bumps on the skull) in the corresponding regions. Gall and his disciple Spurzheim tried to prove this theory by examining the skulls of the inmates of jails and mental hospitals. They claimed to have found, for example, that pickpockets had prominent bumps on the skull in the region associated with the faculty

of 'acquisitiveness'. When Gall died, his skull was examined by one of his followers, who reported: 'The organs of ... Adhesiveness, Combativeness, and Destructiveness were all very well developed in Gall. His Secretiveness was also rather large, but he never made use of it'. Gall was thus hoist with his own phrenological petard. But his theory continued to enjoy an enormous popularity, particularly in Great Britain, where at one time no fewer than 29 phrenological societies flourished, and in the United States. But French physiologists and medical experts were sceptical about phrenology from the start, and it soon collapsed under the weight of accumulating scientific evidence.

Towards the end of the eighteenth century, the French government appointed scientific commissions to look into the work of Mesmer. They found no evidence for 'animal magnetism', or any other physical basis for the trances which Mesmer produced in his patients. The French government is said to have offered him 20,000 francs, a princely sum in those days, to disclose his secret. His inability to oblige — he had no secret — severely damaged his reputation, and he was forced to flee to Switzerland. During the early part of the nineteenth century, it gradually became apparent that hypnotic trances were not epiphenomena of some mysterious physical process. Hypnosis turned out to be a most dramatic example of a purely psychological phenomenon with psychological causes and certain important bodily effects. Simply by suggestion, for example, a hypnotist could cause a part of the subject's body to become anaesthetized. These discoveries were quite incompatible with the doctrine of epiphenomenalism.

While knowledge of the nervous system accumulated during the nineteenth century, mental illnesses without any accompanying physical disorders came to light. The most striking examples were cases of hysteria in which patients suffered blindness, deafness, paralysis, or loss of sensation, without any apparent organic disorder. In the light of existing knowledge of anatomy and physiology, the nature of the symptoms sometimes ruled out the possibility of any simple physical causes of the illnesses. No damage to the nervous system can cause a numbness in the hand without the arm being affected, for example; yet cases of hysterical 'glove anaesthesia' were often reported. Hysteria and other mental illnesses gradually came to be viewed in a similar way to hypnosis, as essentially psychological in nature and origin, but having bodily effects. This view of mental illness made the doctrine of epiphenomenalism increasingly difficult to maintain. The mind-body problem was back with a vengeance.

At about the same time, the commonsense view that mind can influence matter suffered a severe blow from a different quarter. This blow came from the discovery of the first law of thermodynamics, familiar to most people as the law of the conservation of energy. This law was discovered by a German physician called Julius Robert Mayer. His important contribution was rejected by the leading physics journal, *Annalen der Physik*, and was eventually published in 1842 in a less appropriate chemistry journal. As a result, it was ignored by physicists. Deeply distressed by this, Mayer suffered a mental breakdown from which he never recovered during the remaining 30 years of his life. Meanwhile, the law was independently rediscovered in England, and it became widely known after being reported to the Royal Society by the physicist, Lord Kelvin, in 1851.

The essence of the law of the conservation of energy is as

follows: heat, chemical reactions, electricity, or magnetism can be converted into mechanical energy, but such energy cannot be created out of thin air, so to speak. Every physical movement or change in the world involves a transfer of energy. All physical work consumes some form of physical energy and generates an equal amount of energy in another form; this is why rubbing one's hands together consumes food energy and generates warmth. Thus the total amount of energy in the universe remains constant through all these changes. The discovery of this law led to the following inescapable conclusion: physical movements of the body, such as those involved in walking, writing, or rubbing the hands together, cannot be caused by mental processes like thoughts or desires, since mental processes, by definition, belong to a non-physical realm in which heat, chemical reactions, electricity, and magnetism do not exist.

The demise of epiphenomenalism and the discovery of the law of the conservation of energy forced nineteenth century philosophers to find a new solution to the mind-body problem. The solution which became fashionable is known as *psycho-physical parallelism*. This idea had been suggested by the German philosopher, Gottfried Wilhelm Leibniz (1646-1716), in the early eighteenth century. But Leibniz was 100 years ahead of his time, and his suggestion caught on only in the mid-nineteenth century following the developments discussed above.

The central idea of psycho-physical parallelism can be explained quite simply. Mental experiences and certain kinds of physical events occur simultaneously. They may seem to influence each other or to interact, but this is an illusion; in reality the two realms operate quite independently of each other. A physical injury to the foot, or a particular brain process, may be *accompanied* by a distinct mental experience of pain, but it does not actually *cause* it. Neither does any mental process ever *cause* a bodily movement. The illusion of mind-body interaction is similar to the illusion of the two clocks: if a pair of clocks are placed side by side, their movements may seem to be linked in a kind of causal interaction, but they do not really cause each other to move;

each clock in fact moves independently. Minds and bodies do not really interact either; there is simply a strict psycho-physical parallelism between mental experiences and certain kinds of bodily processes such as brain events.

The theory of psycho-physical parallelism was more in keeping with scientific knowledge in the second half of the nineteenth century than were previous theories of mind and body. Without violating the law of the conservation of energy, it explained how mental experiences seemed to cause physical events and how physical events seemed to cause mental experiences. Once psycho-physical parallelism became fashionable, the intellectual climate was favourable for the emergence of psychology as an independent discipline. Mental experiences were no longer looked upon as trivial epiphenomena of brain processes. It became scientifically respectable, for the first time in many decades, to look for psychological causes of psychological processes. The pioneering experimental psychologists of the late nineteenth century were all believers in psycho-physical parallelism. It is doubtful, in fact, whether experimental psychology would have emerged when it did had it not been for the popularlity of this kind of solution to the mind-body problem. The same may be said of Freud's psychoanalytic theory, which he began to develop during this period. Freud was also a psycho-physical parallelist, and his theory rested squarely on the doctrine that psychological phenomena all have psychological causes. Epiphenomenalism, with its peculiar bias against mental experiences, or for that matter Descartes' brand of interactionism, could hardly have hosted the arrival of experimental psychology or psychoanalysis.

In order to understand the actual content and methods of early experimental psychology, it is necessary to consider certain philosophical influences of a different kind. These influences stemmed from nineteenth century British philosophy, particularly the doctrines of *associationism* and *empiricism*. Both of these doctrines can be traced to the writings of John Locke. What follows is a brief discussion of the role which each of them played in the history of psychology.

Newton's *Principia*, which contained his revolutionary theory of gravity, was published in 1687. In 1700, Locke added a chapter entitled 'Of the Association of Ideas' to a revised edition of his *Essay Concerning Human Understanding*, which had first appeared 10 years earlier. This chapter outlined a theory of attraction between mental elements (ideas) in terms which were very reminiscent of those used by Newton to describe the attraction between physical bodies.

Associationism was elaborated into a powerful theory by the early and mid-nineteenth century mental philosophers, James Mill and his son John Stuart Mill. According to the Mills, mental experiences consist of elements of two kinds. *Sensations* (tastes, smells, sights, sounds, and so on) are the elementary experiences we have when our sense organs are stimulated, and *ideas* are the thoughts and images (memories) which we experience in the absence of such physical stimuli. Ideas have a tendency to become associated with one another, and complex ideas arise from the association of simple ideas. When two ideas have become associated with each other, they tend to call each other up; it becomes difficulty or impossible to experience one without the other. The idea of redness, for example, is associated in most people's minds with the idea of warmth, so that we tend to think of warmth whenever we think of redness. This process is held to account for all features of mental experience, which takes the form of a stream of consciousness interrupted only by dreamless sleep and death.

James Mill believed that a single law, later called the *law of contiguity,* was sufficient to account for all mental associations and complex ideas. According to this law, elements become associated when they relate to things which are close to each other (contiguous) in time or space. Redness, for example, is associated with warmth because the two are experienced together in glowing coals and suchlike. John Stuart Mill added further laws of association, such as *similarity* (similar ideas tend to become associated) and *frequency* (the more frequently ideas occur together, the more strongly they become associated). He also abandoned the 'mental mechanics' of his father in favour of 'mental chemistry'. The reason for this suggestion is that complex ideas are not formed by the mechanical combination of simple ideas but, as in chemical reactions, develop quite new properties. The properties of water are qualitatively different from those of its constituent elements, hydrogen and oxygen. In a similar way, John Stuart Mill argued, simple ideas combine to form complex ideas which are qualitatively different from their elements; in other words, a complex idea may not resemble the sum of its parts. The idea of whiteness, for example, can arise from the association, according to the law of contiguity, of all the colours of the rainbow presented together or in rapid succession. (Newton had demonstrated this effect in his *Opticks*.)

Associationist philosophy is reflected in the theories of the early experimental psychologists and psychoanalysts, which are discussed in more detail later in this chapter. John Stuart Mill's suggestion that mental wholes may be different from the sum of their parts became central to the Gestalt school of psychology which later emerged in Germany. Mental chemistry reappeared in a more sophisticated form in the theories of Wundt, the father of modern psychology, and formed the starting-point of the structuralist school of the late nineteenth and early twentieth centuries. Associationist principles were also reflected in the therapeutic methods of Freud and his followers from the turn of the century onwards. Freud's method of *free association* and Jung's *word-association test* (actually invented by the British psychologist Francis Galton in 1883) have their roots in associationist mental philosophy.

A late development in associationist philosophy which had far-reaching consequences for psychology is largely attributable to the Scottish philosopher Alexander Bain. In Bain's version of associationism, the mental elements include not only sensations, ideas, and emotions. He also included elements of a radically different kind, which no previous philosopher had dreamed of considering alongside mental elements, namely movements of the body. Bain distinguished between voluntary movements, and involuntary, automatic types of behaviour, which he called 'instincts' (they later came to be called reflexes). Bodily movements, whether voluntary or instinctual, were thought by Bain to be capable of forming associations with sensations, ideas, and emotions. It was only a short step from this theory to the later psychological theories about associations between physical *stimuli* which evoke sensations and behavioural *responses* which result from such stimulation.

The concepts of *stimulus* and *response*, which were the building blocks of the psychology of the behaviourist school, can be traced to the elements in Bain's associationism. The third important component of behaviourist psychology, the concept of the conditioned reflex, follows naturally from Bain's suggestion that bodily movements can enter into associations with other elements. Bain's influence on early experimental psychology was enormous. He devoted most of his energy to thinking and writing about mental philosophy, and in 1876 founded the journal *Mind*, the first periodical in any country devoted to psychological questions.

Another important philosophical idea first put forward by Locke in his *Essay* was the doctrine of empiricism. The essence of this doctrine is the suggestion that people are born with minds like blank sheets of paper on which their later experiences are written. Everything we come to know, according to this view, is the result of information acquired through the senses and reflection on this information; nothing is innate in the mind.

British empiricism had an important influence on the methods adopted by the early experimental psychologists. It encouraged them to tackle old questions, which had previously been approached only by armchair speculation, by means of new methods based on controlled observations. The doctrine that all knowledge comes ultimately from the senses led Locke and his empiricist successors Berkeley and Hume to formulate the following rule of method: all statements about the world for which evidence is lacking ought to be rejected as valueless; only those which can be verified by observations are worthy of acceptance.

For the nineteenth century mental philosophers, observations of private mental experiences, seen as it were from the inside, counted as empirical evidence. Some of them even argued that introspective observations were more direct, and therefore more trustworthy than observations of external events. The early experimental psychologists focussed their attention mainly on mental experiences: their research was based largely on controlled introspection under experimental conditions. A peculiar twist to the empiricist doctrine was, however, later introduced by psychologists of the behaviourist school. They took the view that only observations of another person's (or animal's) outward behaviour were truly 'scientific'. The behaviourists' anti-mentalistic views can be explained, at least in part, by the fact that they were trying to model psychology on the older and more respected sciences, such as physics and biology. In these branches of science, of course, only publicly observable events were used as empirical evidence.

Biological Roots

The Industrial Revolution, which transformed the economy of northern Europe from around the mid-eighteenth century onwards, was accompanied by dramatic advances in many branches of natural philosophy, or what later became known as natural science. The rejection of explanations based on miracles and magic, and the growth of a more rationalistic world view during this period, fostered scientific research on the structure and function of living things, particularly in England and France. Post-mortem dissections of human bodies, which had been frowned on by the Church for centuries, became more acceptable, and the newly-invented microscope enabled minute inspections to be made of nerves, muscles, and sense organs. During the second half of the eighteenth century the discipline of physiology became established, with numerous investigations being made of simple bodily processes such as reflexes. Towards the end of the century, Luigi Galvani demonstrated that the legs of a frog could be made to move by passing an electrical current through them, thus providing a basis from which the physiology of the nervous system later developed.

By the second decade of the nineteenth century, knowledge of the nervous system had become quite sophisticated. In 1811 the English physiologist, Sir Charles Bell, discovered that the nerves were of two kinds: those which carried information from the sense organs and which entered the spinal column from the back, and those which transmitted impulses to the muscles and were attached to the front of the spinal column. This important finding was made independently by Francois Magendie in France in 1822, and became known as the Bell-Magendie law.

In 1861 and 1865 Paul Broca reported the first scientific evidence linking a psychological function to a specific area of the brain. A series of patients with severe speech defects but normal comprehension of spoken and written language were shown to have suffered damage to an area of the cortex close to the left temple, which subsequently became known as Broca's speech area. In 1874 Carl Wernicke discovered another brain area which is associated with language in a different way. Wernicke's area lies close to the left ear, and lesions in this region were shown to be associated with a loss of *comprehension* of both spoken and written language, rather than any inability to utter recognizable words such as was found in patients with damage to Broca's area. In both classes of patients, hearing of non-verbal sounds and music is unaffected. It is amusing to note that these brain areas had been labelled 'Constructiveness' and 'Secretiveness' in Spurzheim's major textbook of phrenology in 1834; phrenology did have its value, however, in that it stimulated more solid research on the functions of the brain.

In 1850 the German physiologist Hermann von Helmholtz published the first of a series of papers which were to play a vital part in the later development of psychology. Helmholtz's early work was concerned with measuring the speed at which nerve impulses travelled. Nerve conduction had previously been assumed to be instantaneous, but Helmholtz's findings showed that it was in fact rather slow: in the region of one-millionth of the speed of light. He later made important contributions to the physiology of vision and hearing. Helmholtz's teaching assistant at one time was Wilhelm Wundt, who was destined to found the world's first psychological laboratory in Leipzig in 1879. The emphasis which Wundt and the other early experimental psychologists placed on the study of sensation and reaction time was due in large part to the influence of physiological research such as the work of Helmholtz in the late nineteenth century. The development of reflexology in Russia and the emergence of the behaviourist school in the United States in the early twentieth century also owe a great deal to this physiological heritage, based as they were on investigations of reflex arcs.

A different kind of biological influence on the early development of psychology came from the theory of evolution. Evolutionary ideas were very much in vogue during the mid-nineteenth century, and they gained enormous impetus after the publication in 1859 of Charles Darwin's *The Origin of Species by Means of Natural Selection, or the Preservation of Favoured Races in the Struggle for Life.* Darwin's theory regarding the variety of biological species on earth offered a natural mechanism in place of earlier theological explanations. The fundamental idea is heredity: offspring reproduce parent organisms fairly faithfully. But small variations occur as a result of accidental hereditary mutations. Occasionally, these new forms happen to be better adapted than others to the environment in which they live; they therefore thrive and produce more offspring bearing the favourable hereditary mutation than do other similar forms which lack it. By means of what became known as 'the survival of the fittest', the great variety of species was thus explained by Darwin as the result of gradual evolution from a single (or perhaps a few) ancestors.

Despite fierce opposition from the Church, Darwin's alternative to the book of Genesis had an impact throughout the scientific community. The mechanistic assumptions underlying the theory harmonized with the then fashionable mode of scientific thinking. The theory appealed to Victorian readers also because it offered a natural model of the competitive economic system of capitalism which had recently emerged from the Industrial Revolution in Europe: in the struggle for economic survival, only the most efficient business enterprises would survive.

The influence of evolutionary thinking in biology on the development of early psychology was enormous. First, the prospect of empirical research rather than theological or philosophical speculation about animal behaviour gripped the imagination. Human beings were viewed for the first time as part of the animal kingdom, though at a 'higher' level of evolutionary development than other species. It had previously been taken for granted that humans were in some important way quite unlike animals through their unique possession of a soul; Descartes, for example, believed that animals were merely machines. Second, individual differences between people became, for the first time, a topic of serious enquiry. Since it was in intellectual capacity rather than, for example, in physical strength or agility that humans were supposed to be evolutionarily superior to other animals, early research on individual differences focussed primarily on differences in intelligence. In 1869 Francis Galton, a younger half-cousin of Darwin's, published

Hereditary Genius: An Enquiry Into its Laws and Consequences, which purported to show that intelligence was hereditary by investigating the family trees of nearly 1000 eminent British judges, statesmen, commanders, literary men, men of science, poets, artists, divines, and even oarsmen and wrestlers. When he found that eminence tends to run in families to a greater extent than would be expected on the basis of chance alone, he took this as overwhelming evidence that ability is hereditary. This book also contains a chapter, the first of its kind in psychological literature, on 'The Comparative Worth of Different Races'. Galton later made an unsuccessful attempt to develop an objective intelligence test, and he laid the groundwork of an important branch of statistics for analysing the results of such tests. He is largely responsible for introducing into psychology the ideas of individual and group differences in intelligence, psychometrics in general and intelligence testing in particular, and statistical methods of data analysis. His influence can be traced in the history of British psychology through his disciple Karl Pearson and successive psychologists of the London school, such as Charles Spearman, Sir Cyril Burt, and Hans Eysenck.

The third way in which evolutionary ideas penetrated into psychology was in the form of an analogy. The early behaviourists interpreted learning as a process in which 'accidental' elements of behaviour are selectively 'conditioned' through association; eventually only the most successful elements survive and are strengthened. This whole process can be thought of as a kind of natural selection. Members of the functionalist school, for their part, interpreted virtually all behaviour from the point of view of its usefulness in the 'struggle for life'. The influence of evolutionary ideas is less obvious in the other schools of psychology, which originated in non-English-speaking countries where Darwin's ideas had not penetrated so deeply.

The Emergence of the Discipline

The prevailing intellectual currents in philosophy and biology in the late nineteenth century encouraged the drift of scholarly thinking towards psychology. Mental philosophy was flourishing once again alongside natural philosophy. The desirability and feasibility of experimental investigations of mental functioning became increasingly apparent. Scientific discoveries in related fields suggested avenues of research which might produce valuable insights about sensation, the association of ideas, reaction times, and reflexes, to mention but a few of the more obvious psychological processes.

Against this intellectual background, psychology finally emerged as an independent discipline in Germany in the 1880s. The date which most historians choose for the birth of experimental psychology is 1879, the year in which Wilhelm Wundt's laboratory was established in Leipzig. Within a decade, psychology was a going concern in several parts of Germany. Myths abound about the origins of psychology; it is worth pausing for a moment to consider exactly what happened (and what did not happen) in Germany in the 1880s.

The attempt to understand the human mind and behaviour was, as we have seen, nothing new. Important contributions in this area had already been made long before the time of Plato and Aristotle. Nor was the word *psychology* an invention of the nineteenth century. In the second edition of *Blancard's Physical Dictionary*, published in English in 1693, *Anthropologia,* the 'description of man' is divided into '*Anatomy*, which treats of the Body, and *Psychology*, which treats of the Soul'. In his *Observations on Man,* published in 1748, David Hartley, the English associationist philosopher, used the word *psychology* for the first time in its more modern sense to refer to 'the Theory of the human Mind with that of the intellectual Principles of Brute Animals'. By the mid-nineteenth century, this word had become a commonplace synonym for mental philosophy. Not even the use of experimental methods for investigating psychological phenomena was the unique contribution of the early German experimental psychologists. Experiments had been applied to psychological problems throughout the nineteenth century by philosophers, biologists, physicians, and amateurs, including the following representatives of each category: Fechner, Helmholtz, Magendie, and Galton.

The two important historical developments which distinguished psychology in Germany in the 1880s from what had preceded it were, first, the recognition of an independent branch of knowledge in experimental psychology, and second, the formation of a self-conscious and organized community of psychological specialists. Wundt was in the vanguard of the first of these historical movements, but was not at all associated with the latter.

The opening sentence of the preface to Wundt's first major textbook of experimental psychology, published in 1873, reads: 'The work which I here present to the public is an attempt to mark out a new domain of science'. He was well aware that experimental psychology of great importance had already been published. In his own home town of Leipzig, the physiologist Ernst Heinrich Weber and the philosopher-mystic Gustav Theodor Fechner had carried out impressive experimental work. Their results, published in 1846 and 1860, established a fundamental law relating the physical intensity of stimuli to the psychological magnitude of sensation in the area of psychology which is still referred to as *psychophysics*. But Weber considered psychophysics to be a branch of physiology and Fechner thought of it as a contribution to philosophy; Wundt was the first to recognize experimental psychology as a 'new domain of science'.

The emergence of experimental psychology as a discipline in its own right was soon followed by an attempt on the part of the younger German psychologists to establish an organized professional community. This tendency was vigorously opposed by Wundt, and the German Psychological Association was unable to meet in Leipzig until after his death. The professionalization of psychology in Germany was not nearly as rapid and thorough as in the

United States, where its philosophical roots were not so deeply entrenched. Starting with William James' laboratory in Harvard, psychological research centres sprang up in many parts of the United States in the late nineteenth and early twentieth centuries, and American psychologists were quickly organized into a powerful professional society. The bulk of psychological research and publication nevertheless remained centred in Germany until the First World War, and German psychology continued to thrive as an academic discipline until the rise of the Nazi dictatorship in the 1930s.

The development of psychology in France and England, the 'natural' cradles of psychology from an historical point of view, was considerably slower. In France, the materialist and anti-psychological bias introduced during the Enlightenment was never completely eradicated; vestigal materialist tendencies retarded development in most areas apart from physiological and medical psychology. In addition, the rational approach to mental philosophy introduced by Descartes was not replaced by the empirical to the same extent in France as elsewhere. In England, the conservative and ecclesiastical educational policies of the universities of Oxford and Cambridge created an atmosphere hostile to contemporary trends in both the

humanities and the sciences: many of the great English scientists of the nineteenth century, including Darwin and Galton, were amateurs of independent means who worked outside the institutional framework of the university system. In 1877 the Senate of Cambridge University turned down a proposal to establish a psychological laboratory on the grounds that it would 'insult religion by putting the human soul in a pair of scales'. At Oxford, psychology was not taught as a degree subject until 1946, and the holder of the only teaching post in mental philosophy in the early twentieth century (William McDougall) was officially forbidden to experiment; he was expected to adopt a purely speculative approach. Even the new university of London, which was founded in 1836 and was only the third university in the country, was distinctly conservative in its administrative and scientific attitudes. In 1837, for example, John Elliotson successfully treated several patients suffering from nervous complaints by means of hypnosis, but the Council of University College immediately passed a resolution forbidding the practice, and Elliotson resigned from the college and never entered its precincts again. In 1842 W.S. Ward reported the amputation of a leg of a patient under hypnotic anaesthesia to the Royal Medical and Chirugial Society; the Society did not like this at all, and all record of Ward's paper was ordered to be struck from the minutes of the meeting! It is hardly surprising that the new discipline of psychology was slow in penetrating the English academic and scientific establishment.

The Era of Schools

From the end of the nineteenth century until the 1930s, psychology was fragmented into a number of more or less independent schools which were at odds with one another on theoretical issues, research methods, and the kinds of psychological phenomena which they chose to study. Structuralism and functionalism sprang up as immediate products of the philosophical and biological antecedents of psychology, particularly associationist philosophy and evolutionary theory respectively. Behaviourism and Gestalt psychology arose initially as revolts against the theories and methods of other schools. Psychoanalysis developed independently in a medical rather than an academic context.

163

By the end of the Second World War the schools had declined, although psychoanalysis continued as an organized profession outside the mainstream of academic psychology, and a modified form of neo-behaviourism remained influential in American universities. But in spite of the decline of the schools, current areas of psychological research retain unmistakable characteristics of the theories and methods of the early part of the century.

Structuralism. The most important sources of structuralist psychology were Wundt's *Outline of Psychology,* first published in Germany in 1896, and a book by Edward Bradford Titchener which bore the same title and was published in the United States in the same year. Titchener was born in England and studied philosophy at Oxford. From 1890 to 1892 he was in Leipzig studying under Wundt, and the last 35 years of his life, from 1892 to 1927, were spent at Cornell University in the United States, where he attracted a considerable following.

The structuralists attempted to study mental life by analysing its elements, their properties, and the way they combine or become associated with one another. The most important elements were sensations, but some attention was also given to ideas (images of memory or imagination) and feelings. The chief method of investigation involved introspection (observation by an individual of his own mental processes) by trained subjects under experimental conditions. Wundt restricted his experimental work to the investigation of simple mental elements. Complex thought processes, including those involving language, he classified as social psychology and investigated by non-experimental methods, particularly by examing their products in primitive cultures. Titchener, and also the younger German psychologists such as Külpe and Ebbinghaus, repudiated this distinction and brought 'higher mental processes' into the ambit of experimental psychology. Ebbinghaus, for example, was the pioneer of experimental research on verbal memory in the mid-1880s.

Structuralism declined in Germany with the advent of Nazism in the 1930s, and it disappeared from the American scene shortly after Titchener's death in 1927. Current research on sensation, particularly in the area of psychophysics, is, however, strongly coloured by its structuralist heritage.

Functionalism. The functionalist school was launched in an article by the American philosopher and psychologist John Dewey in 1896. It thrived for a considerable period at Chicago University, under the influence of Dewey, George Herbert Mead, and others, and at Columbia University, where Edward Thorndike and Robert Woodworth were its most influential spokesmen. It arose out of a deliberate attempt to introduce evolutionary ideas into psychology. Instead of attempting to unravel the structure of mental life, the functionalists investigated both mental experiences and behaviour from the point of view of their functional value in adapting the organism to its environment. Following the distinction in biology between the structure and function of living things, they distinguished between the content and function of mental life. They put forward the interesting idea that conscious experiences arise in situations where automatic, reflex behaviour is inadequate to meet the needs of the organism. Once we have learned to ride a bicycle, for example, the skilled movements become habitual, and the need for conscious control grows less and less until it finally disappears. According to the functionalists, consciousness came through evolution to serve the kind of instrumental function of learning to ride a bicycle. The functionalists were the first to treat the behaviour of animals as part of the subject matter of experimental psychology: Thorndike, for example, invented a puzzle box for investigating problem-solving in cats and dogs. Their successors were also the first American psychologists to devote serious attention to individual differences. The research methods used by the functionalists included observations of behaviour and — in the case of humans — introspection.

As behaviourism gained momentum in the 1920s and 1930s, functionalism gradually disappeared from American psychology, and many of its ideas and methods were absorbed into this younger and more powerful school.

165

Current research on thinking and problem-solving owes something to its functionalist pioneers, but the most important legacy of functionalism is the study of individual differences, which later gave birth to psychometrics and the IQ testing movement.

Behaviourism. In 1913 John Broadus Watson broke away from the functionalist school in an article which gave birth to behaviourism. In the succeeding decades, behaviourism gained enormous influence throughout American psychology. The theoretical goal of psychology, according to Watson, is 'the prediction and control of behavior'. This doctrine represented a complete rejection of the classical experimental psychology of the structuralists, which involved neither prediction nor control nor behaviour.

The introspectionist methods of the structuralists and functionalists were discarded by Watson as unscientific, and everything except the behaviour of people and animals was excluded from the subject matter of psychology. Mental processes like thinking were declared to be nothing but small-scale movements of the vocal apparatus, and emotion was nothing but the secretion of glands; that is to say, both thinking and feeling were reinterpreted as special kinds of 'behaviour'. The doctrine of *operationalism* was borrowed from positivist philosophy: according to this doctrine, the meaning of scientific concepts is simply the set of operations through which they are measured. Thus, for example, intelligence is what IQ tests measure; it can have no other scientific meaning.

According to the behaviourists, all behaviour can be explained in terms of a particular kind of learning based on *conditioned reflexes.* Conditioned reflexes are simple associations between elements arising from the law of contiguity of the associationist philosophers (elements which are closely associated in time or place tend to combine) but the behaviourist elements are the physical stimuli which excite the sense organs and the bodily responses of the organism. Watson was probably not familiar with the work of the Russian reflexologists such as Ivan Pavlov when he developed his conditioning theory. But

Pavlov's famous conditioning experiments, in which hungry dogs were made to salivate to the sound of a bell by the repeated pairing of the sound with food, added further impetus to the behaviourist movement when they became known in the United States.

Since the late 1930s, the most influential proponent of neo-behaviourist doctrines has been the American psychologist Burrhus Skinner. These doctrines have lost much of their force in the face of mounting contradictory evidence from various sources and attacks on positivist dogmas. But neo-behaviourist ideas and methods nevertheless form the basis of current research in the area of learning.

Gestalt psychology. The Gestalt school emerged with the publication of a paper on *apparent movement* by Max Wertheimer in Germany in 1912. Wertheimer was struck by certain features of a visual illusion which he called the *phi phenomenon.* If two light sources close together in an otherwise dark room are switched on and off in an alternating pattern, then, under certain conditions, the powerful illusion is created of a single light moving back and forth. (The 'certain conditions' are determined by the brightness of the lights, their distance apart, and the time gap; they can be precisely specified for all observers in terms of Korte's laws, and make possible cinema and television pictures in which the illusion of movement is created by a very rapid succession of 'still' shots.)

The significance of the phi phenomenon is that it provides a vivid example of a mental experience which cannot be explained in terms of the elementary sensations which give rise to it: the whole (Gestalt) is different from the sum of its parts. The Gestalt psychologists in Germany and Austria, particularly Max Wertheimer, Kurt Koffka, and Wolfgang Köhler, objected to the analytical approach of the structuralists. Mental life, they thought, could never be understood by analysing its elements. They were strongly influenced by the work of the physicist Max Planck on electromagnetic fields; the striking thing about force fields in physics is that they cannot be understood by focussing on

167

details. What is important to an understanding of mental life, the Gestaltists believed, is not the elementary sensations themselves, but the relations between them. The following eight notes, played evenly on a musical instrument, are instantly recognized by most people as the well-known folk tune *Frère Jacques*: C, D, E, C, C, D, E, C. But the tune which is perceived does not depend in any simple way on the elements: the following series of notes sounds like exactly the same tune: F, G, A, F, F, G, A, F, although it does not share a single element in common with the first series. On the other hand, the series: C, C, E, E, D, D, C, C, which contains the same elements as the first series in a new configuration, evokes a completely different melody. The point of all this is that, according to the Gestalt psychologists, an analytic investigation of the elements of consciousness cannot reveal the important facts of mental life. To understand the mind, we need to study overall patterns, configurations, or wholes (*Gestalten*) rather than elements.

The influence of Gestalt ideas in Germany receded with the rise of Nazism. Wertheimer, Koffka, and Köhler emigrated to the United States in the 1920s and 1930s, by which time behaviourism, an extreme form of elementalism, had gained a strong foothold there. But in the field of perception certain Gestalt ideas turned out to be irresistible, and contemporary research on perception retains a distinctly Gestalt flavour.

Psychoanalysis. The fundamental ideas of the psychoanalytic school, which grew up around Sigmund Freud in Vienna from the 1890s onwards, have been outlined in Chapter 1. In the present context it is necessary only to add a few words about the social origins of this school, which distinguish it from the others which have been discussed. Wundt and Titchener; Dewey, Thorndike, and the other functionalists; Watson, Wertheimer, Koffka, and Köhler were all academic psychologists. Their aim was to understand — or, in Watson's case, to predict and control — psychological processes. Freud, on the other hand, was a physician whose psychoanalytic couch was inhabited by a continuous stream of neurotic patients in need of urgent treatment; his primary task was to find a way of relieving his patients' crippling neuroses. His therapeutic methods were far removed from the experimental techniques of the academic laboratories, and his theories were not very amenable to experimental testing. His successors, including Carl Gustav Jung, Alfred Adler, and Melanie Klein, were also medical people.

Although the psychoanalytic school rapidly grew large, well-organized, and powerful, it never really gained a footing in the citadels of academic psychology, although the indirect influence of Freud's brilliantly original ideas on psychological theory is incalculable. It is hardly surprising, in view of the character of the theory and its social origins, that its influence has been most strongly felt in the areas of psychopathology, emotion and motivation, and states of awareness (dreaming and hypnosis in particular).

Further Reading

The classic history of psychology is Boring, E.G. *A History of Experimental Psychology*, 2nd ed. (New York: Appleton-Century-Crofts, 1957). But this book is structured according to 'great psychologists' in a manner which tends to obscure the historical development of ideas, and it is occasionally unreliable on points of detail. R.S. Peters' edition of *Brett's History of Psychology* (London: Allen and Unwin, 1953) is a deeper and more scholarly work, particularly in its treatment of early ideas, but it is not easy to read. A short and easily accessible introduction to the history of psychology is Thomson, R. *The Pelican History of Psychology* (Harmondsworth: Penguin, 1968).

The best way of becoming acquainted with the history of psychology is undoubtedly by reading the key texts at first hand. Important ideas are usually expressed more clearly and emphatically by their originators than by later interpreters. A number of volumes containing selections from historically important psychological writings are available; among them are the following: Dennis, W. (ed.) *Readings in the History of*

Psychology (New York: Appleton-Century-Crofts, 1948); and Watson, R.I. (ed.) *Basic Writings in the History of Psychology* (New York: Oxford University Press, 1979).

6. Psychology as a Profession

The most striking development in psychology since the Second World War has been the emergence of a large number of fields of applied psychology. Before the war, virtually all psychologists were employed as teachers and researchers, and psychology was practised almost exclusively as an academic discipline. Today, more than half of the psychologists in the United States, Britain, and other advanced industrial societies earn their livings by working in applied fields. Applied psychology has grown rapidly in recent decades, and this trend is likely to continue for some time yet.

Historically, the term *applied psychology* used to refer to what is nowadays called *industrial psychology*; the earliest textbooks of applied psychology dealt with personnel selection, efficiency of work, and advertizing. Since the 1950s, however, a number of new fields of applied psychology have emerged. A wider range of careers involving quite different kinds of work is now available to psychology graduates than to graduates in almost any other subject. Most of the careers open to psychologists, however, require some postgraduate training in addition to a first degree, and competition for places on postgraduate courses and for jobs is in some cases quite intense. The routes available to those who wish to become psychologists are outlined later in this chapter. Before enquiring into the details of training, however, most readers will probably wish to have some idea of the kinds of work for which this training qualifies them. The bulk of this chapter is therefore devoted to describing the major activities of pure and applied psychologists.

Psychologists in most advanced industrial societies work in a wide range of settings, including universities and colleges, hospitals, clinics, community and counselling agencies, consulting and research organizations, schools, prisons, government departments, and commercial and industrial companies. Still others are self-employed in private practice. The proportions of psychologists employed in these various settings differ from one country to another. The patterns of employment of American and British psychologists, estimated from the records of the professional associations in these two countries, are given below.

Most of the qualified psychologists in the United States belong to the American Psychological Association (APA). Founded in 1892, the APA has approximately 50,000 members and is by far the largest professional society of psychologists in the world. Roughly 47 per cent of its members are employed as teachers and researchers in universities, colleges, and other institutions of higher learning. About 21 per cent work as clinical or counselling psychologists in hospitals, clinics, and counselling agencies of various kinds, and a further 9 per cent are engaged in private practice doing similar work. Approximately 9 per cent are employed as psychology teachers or school psychologists in the American school system. A further 5 per cent work for various government agencies and military institutions, and 5 per cent are employed by consulting and research organizations. Approximately 3 per cent are employed directly by private commercial and industrial companies.

The British Psychological Society (BPS), founded in 1901 and incorporated by Royal Charter in 1965, has almost 10,000 members. Roughly 30 per cent of British psychologists are employed as teachers and researchers in universities, polytechnics, and colleges. Close to 15 per cent are employed as clinical psychologists in the National Health Service. A similar proportion — about 15 per cent — are educational psychologists working for local education authorities either in Child Guidance Clinics or in School

Psychological Services. Approximately 8 per cent are occupational or industrial psychologists employed by the government or by private companies. An unknown but probably substantial proportion of British psychologists pursue careers which are only indirectly related to psychology, such as school teaching and social work.

The figures given above refer to qualified psychologists only. In many parts of the world, services of a pseudo-psychological kind are sold by people who have no formal qualifications in psychology. Various exotic forms of therapy purporting to cure emotional and sexual problems are widely advertized, and courses are offered which promise to improve self-confidence, memory, concentration, popularity, self-awareness, interpersonal sensitivity, social skills, bodily awareness, and selling ability, to name but a few. Some of the pseudo-psychological services which are available obviously satisfy real needs and provide genuine benefits to those who partake of them. But others are quite valueless — except to those who profit financially by providing them — and some are positively harmful in their effects. The problem of charlatanism is particularly acute in applied psychology for two reasons. First, the various fields of applied psychology are of recent origin; until the 1950s few properly trained psychologists worked outside the framework of the universities or provided services of a practical nature. Second, there is still widespread misunderstanding of the true nature of psychology; members of the public are insufficiently informed to be able to distinguish between genuine and spurious psychology.

In some countries, this problem has been dealt with in a limited way by the legal registration, certification, or licensing of applied psychologists. In the United States, for example, most state legislatures have introduced either certification laws which forbid practitioners who are not properly qualified from calling themselves 'psychologists', or licensing laws which define certain psychological services and make it illegal for unqualified people to offer these services for payment. Legal registration of psychologists in one form or another exists in many other countries, including Canada, Australia, New Zealand, South Africa, Norway, Sweden, and Japan. In Britain, the issue is currently under discussion, and some form of legal registration is likely to come into force in the near future.

Applied psychologists generally favour legal control. This is hardly surprising, since it is clearly in their own professional self-interests: in the United States, one of the effects of certification and licensing laws has been to inhibit or suppress competition from pseudo-psychologists. The arguments which are usually put forward in favour of legal control are based upon the protection of the public from the activities of inadequately trained people calling themselves 'psychologists' and offering services of an essentially psychological nature. There are those, however, who reject the implication that psychologists have a monopoly of knowledge or skills which uniquely qualifies them to dispense psychological services. According to this view, much of the work done by applied psychologists is not based on any arcane or technical knowledge, and the more severe forms of legal control serve only to encourage restrictive practices which are not in the public interest. The debate revolves around the question of who should be allowed to practise psychology; most people agree that only properly qualified people should be allowed to call themselves psychologists.

Teaching and Basic Research

Teaching posts in psychology are available in universities and various other institutions of higher or further education. In some countries in which psychology is a recognized school subject, including the United States and Britain, teaching posts in psychology are also available in some secondary schools.

Psychologists teaching at degree level are normally expected to devote themselves mainly or solely to the areas in which they specialize. A specialist in developmental psychology, for example, is not normally required to teach physiological psychology, sensation and perception, or any other topic far removed from developmental psychology, except occasionally at the most elementary level. Psychologists attached to colleges and other institutions offering more general courses are often expected to cover a much wider range of teaching topics. This applies particularly to psychology teachers in schools. In other cases, the range of topics is determined to a large extent by the nature of the courses being offered. Some psychologists teaching in higher education, for example, are not employed in psychology departments; they may be attached to departments of sociology, social work, education, management studies, political science, communication studies, or one of the other disciplines in which certain aspects of psychology are taught.

Teaching, in one form or another, takes up a substantial proportion of the working time of most university psychologists, and an even larger proportion of the working time of psychology teachers in other kinds of institutions. One of the most common methods of teaching in higher

education involves lecturing to large groups of students. Most lecturers use fairly detailed notes, which they keep up to date by consulting books and journal articles in the fields in which they are required to teach, and by attending conferences at which researchers report their latest discoveries. Other commonly used teaching methods are seminars with medium-sized groups of students, and tutorials which may involve small-group or individual

175

tuition. Psychologists teaching at degree level are also frequently involved in running laboratory classes, and in supervising the research projects and dissertations of undergraduate and postgraduate students up to the doctoral level. This kind of tuition is done on a one-to-one basis.

In addition to their teaching duties, and various administrative tasks connected with the running of their departments, university psychologists are usually required, in the terms of their contracts of employment, to carry out research. Non-university psychology teachers are not always expected to do research, and in practice most of the basic research which is published in the leading psychological journals is done by university teachers based in psychology departments. It is not essential to be employed in a psychology department, or for that matter in an institution of higher education in order to carry out basic research; in theory, anyone can do it. Psychology departments are, however, ideal environments for this kind of activity on account of the facilities which they provide, such as computers and other items of hardware, expert technicians, and easy access to psychological journals.

In order to perform original research, a psychologist needs first of all to become familiar with the work which has been done by others in some chosen area of investigation. A familiarity with the 'state of the art' in a particular area may reveal certain unanswered questions which call for further investigation. A strenuous exercise of the imagination and a measure of good luck are usually needed in order to choose a line of investigation which is likely to prove fruitful, and to design an appropriate study. Very often, it is necessary to persuade an external grant-giving body that the proposed research is likely to provide valuable answers in order to attract the financial support necessary to carry it out. If the research turns out to be successful, the investigator or investigators (research projects are often collaborative efforts) may decide to submit their results in the form of a manuscript to an appropriate psychological journal. The manuscript will then be read by referees chosen by the journal editor on the basis of their expert knowledge of the particular area of investigation. In the light of the referees' reports, the editor will decide whether the manuscript is of a sufficiently high standard to merit publication. Many of the best psychological journals reject more than 80 per cent of the manuscripts which are submitted to them. If the referees report favourably on the manuscript, the investigators are eventually rewarded by seeing their work published.

Teaching and basic research do not suit all psychologists. Psychology is a rapidly changing subject, and continuous effort is required in order to keep abreast of current developments. Many psychologists employed in higher educational institutions find it difficult to strike the right balance between teaching and research, and between reading and writing. Nevertheless, teaching posts in psychology, particularly in universities, are highly sought after, and competition for jobs is very keen. The chief attractions are probably the relative freedom given to an employee to pursue his or her own interests, and the relaxed and informal working conditions.

Applicants for teaching posts at degree level are usually evaluated according to their formal qualifications, publications, and experience. The conditions of supply and demand for psychology teaching at other levels vary a great deal, but in most cases a good first degree in psychology is essential, and in many a higher degree is required. Psychology teachers in schools are normally expected to have a recognized teaching qualification.

Clinical, Counselling and Community Psychology

The careers discussed in this section all involve helping people with various problems which they encounter in their daily lives. Clinical psychologists deal with people who are believed to be suffering from psychological disorders, such as anxiety states, depression, phobias, or schizophrenia. They are generally employed in hospitals and clinics alongside psychiatrists, but some are in private practice. Counselling psychologists offer assistance to people who are faced with problems of a generally non-clinical nature; they are usually employed by counselling services in universities and other educational institutions, or by specialized counselling agencies of various kinds. Community psychologists deal with similar problems to those of clinical and counselling psychologists, but they operate at a community rather than an individual level; they work chiefly for community organizations, social services, and welfare agencies.

A large part of the work of a clinical psychologist centres on psychological assessment. Upon seeing a patient or client for the first time, the initial task facing the clinical psychologist is invariably one of trying to understand the nature of the person's problem. This usually involves interviewing the person in depth about all matters which might relate directly or indirectly to the problem. During these initial interviews, the clinician pays close attention to what the person has to say, trying to 'read between the lines' where necessary, and also to various aspects of non-verbal behaviour which might provide further relevant information about the person's feelings. Very often, it becomes apparent at an early stage that the problem is quite different from how it was described initially.

Clinical psychologists make considerable use of psychological tests which are designed to assist in the assessment of psychological disorders. The best of these instruments are psychometric tests which have been standardized on large samples of psychiatric and non-psychiatric groups in order to establish norms and to ensure reliability and validity. Psychometric tests can be particularly helpful in answering questions such as the following: 'Is this child mentally handicapped?'; 'Is there any evidence for brain damage in this man?'; 'What is the nature of this woman's psychological disorder?'. Other sources of information which clinical psychologists use in assessment include reports from relatives, nurses, general practitioners, and other people acquainted with the patients or clients, and diaries which the latter may be requested to write. A clinical psychologist's assessment is often only one contribution among those of the members of a team involved with the case, which may include nurses, psychiatrists, and social workers.

Perhaps the most important part of a clinical psychologist's work involves therapy with individuals or groups. The major therapeutic methods may be divided, rather arbitrarily and with some overlap, into three categories: verbal psychotherapy, behaviour therapy, and group therapy. Verbal psychotherapy involves methods of dealing with people's problems through talking. There are numerous different techniques of verbal psychotherapy; only a few of the most widely used techniques can be dealt with here. To begin with, there are the psychoanalytic methods based upon the writings of Freud. Between 10 and 20 per cent of American clinical psychologists use essentially psychoanalytic methods of therapy; the proportion in Britain is considerably smaller. The most distinctive feature of this type of therapy is the attempt which is made to interpret the unconscious sources of people's psychological problems. The basic techniques of psychoanalytic therapy were outlined in Chapter 1.

Another popular technique of verbal psychotherapy is *client-centred therapy*, based on the work of the American psychologist Carl Rogers. In sharp contrast to psychoanalytic techniques, the client-centred therapist refrains from making any interpretations, and from probing, advising, suggesting, or persuading. This approach is therefore also known as non-directive therapy or counselling. The basic assumption is that people are potentially able to identify the sources of their emotional problems and work out effective solutions for themselves once they are freed from feelings of anxiety and insecurity. To encourage this, the therapist tries to establish genuine empathy with the client and to convey an attitude of 'unconditional positive regard', in an attempt to create a permissive, accepting, non-threatening relationship in which the client can come to grips with the problem. The therapist assists by clarifying, re-phrasing, and reflecting back the feelings which lie behind the client's verbal statements. A client may, for example, declare: 'This is just a waste of time. I feel just as depressed as I did last week.' A client-centred therapist might reply: 'You feel frustrated and angry because the therapy doesn't seem to be having any effect.'

A technique of verbal psychotherapy which is based on a fundamentally different set of assumptions is *rational-emotive therapy*, pioneered by the American psychologist Albert Ellis. Rational-emotive therapists believe that psychological disorders are caused by the way people interpret events in their lives, rather than by the events themselves. It is only when these interpretations are irrational that psychological disorders arise. A person who is rejected in love, for example, may (quite rationally) believe that he or she is unfortunate or unlucky, in which case feelings of regret, frustration, or irritation may arise. But if the rejection is (irrationally) interpreted as proof that he or she is a worthless, unlovable, or even hateful person, then feelings of extreme anxiety or depression may arise, and a neurosis may be in the making. The rational-emotive therapist challenges the irrational aspects of people's belief systems in an extremely directive manner. An attempt is made to persuade the client to adopt more rational beliefs, through suggestion, argument, homework assignments, and many other special techniques.

The methods of *behaviour therapy* (or behaviour modification) are more extensively used by clinical psychologists in Britain than are any other therapeutic techniques, and they are rapidly gaining ground in other countries. The fundamental assumptions of behaviour therapists are that most kinds of psychological disorders can be interpreted as maladaptive patterns of behaviour which result from learning processes, and that similar processes may be used in the unlearning of these behaviour patterns or in the learning of more appropriate ones. Behaviour therapists believe that to eliminate the symptoms is to eliminate the disorder: they reject the notion of hidden causes such as is found in psychoanalytic theory. This approach to the causes and cures of psychological disorders has its roots in the work of John B. Watson, the founder of behaviourism (see Chapter 5). Two illustrative examples from among the many behaviour therapy techniques in common use are outlined below.

A behaviour therapy technique which is believed to be extremely effective in treating phobias (unreasonable and debilitating fears of spiders, open spaces, heights, strangers, and the like), developed in the 1950s by the South African psychiatrist Joseph Wolpe, is known as *systematic desensitization.* This is a counter-conditioning technique in which the phobic stimulus (eg spiders) is repeatedly paired with a response which is physiologically incompatible with

anxiety, such as deep muscular relaxation. The technique is essentially as follows. First, the therapist helps the client to draw up a hierarchy of increasingly anxiety-producing imaginary situations involving the phobic stimulus. The hierarchy may range, for example, from (1) 'My child shows me a drawing she has made of a spider's web', to (10) 'I wake up in the middle of the night to find a spider crawling slowly into my mouth.' Next, the client is taught how to enter a state of deep muscular relaxation. (Up to half a dozen therapeutic sessions may be devoted to hierarchy construction and relaxation training before the therapy proper begins.) Finally, the client is placed in a relaxed state and encouraged to visualize the lowest item on the hierarchy as vividly as possible without becoming tense. At the slightest feeling of tension or anxiety, the client raises a finger, whereupon he or she is instructed to banish the image, and relaxation is reinstated. When the client can repeatedly visualize the lowest item on the hierarchy without tension or anxiety, the second item is attempted. With the therapist's assistance, the client works slowly up the hierarchy until the most anxiety-provoking item can be visualized repeatedly without loss of deep muscular relaxation. There is evidence to show that systematic desensitization often results in decreased anxiety in real life situations in which the phobic stimuli are encountered, although there is a great deal of controversy about *how* and *why* it works.

A somewhat different behaviour therapy technique, based on the *operant conditioning* work of Burrhus F. Skinner (see the answer to Question 14 in Chapter 2), is used most often with severely mentally handicapped people, autistic children, and psychiatric patients suffering from severe psychotic disorders such as schizophrenia. This form of therapy is essentially a method of training through reinforcement or reward. A child with severely retarded language development may, for example, be exposed to lengthy training sessions, during which the therapist shapes the child's verbal behaviour by rewarding with chocolates after successive approximations to recognizable speech sounds, then words, then phrases, and finally sentences. In hospital wards for severe schizophrenics, 'token economies' are sometimes established. In a token economy, a patient's access to desirable objects or activities (reinforcements), such as special foods, cigarettes, or television sets, is made contingent upon the performance of certain 'target' behaviour patterns, such as dressing or speaking 'normally' or reading a newspaper. In order to receive the reinforcements, a patient has to accumulate tokens which are given out by the ward staff whenever target behaviour patterns are observed. Token economies have been shown to lead to increases in 'normal' behaviour, but some clinical psychologists consider such methods to be ethically questionable on account of their highly manipulative character.

The final category of therapeutic methods widely used by clinical psychologists consists of various *group therapy* techniques. These techniques range from traditional group therapies, based on the various methods described above but conducted in groups, to the more recent encounter, sensitivity, marathon, growth, confrontation, and gestalt group therapies, whose aims and methods are somewhat different. It is impossible to give an adequate summary of these techniques here. The essential idea which lies behind most of them may, however, be stated quite simply. It is this: if a group of people meets on a regular basis under the guidance of a therapist, and if the members of the group are encouraged to relate to one another in an open and forthright manner, then various benefits may accrue to the participants. Feelings of isolation may give way to a sense of emotional support. People may view their own problems in a new perspective once they become aware of the intimate problems of others. Feedback from other group members may provide an individual with an insight into the way he or she appears to others which never emerges from ordinary social interactions. And people may learn, for the first time, how to express emotions and how to trust others. Many of the newer group therapies involve interpersonal games and activities calculated to foster trust, self-awareness, and interpersonal sensitivity. They lie largely outside the mainstream of clinical psychology, and many professionals are more than a little sceptical about their therapeutic efficacy (for which evidence is still largely lacking), but other less conservative clinical psychologists adopt a more favourable attitude towards some of them.

Counselling psychology, which developed into an active field of applied psychology during the 1950s and 1960s, is a modern descendant of the vocational guidance movement of earlier decades. But contemporary counselling psychologists are involved in helping people to make decisions and solve problems in a number of areas of life apart from career choices. Counselling work overlaps to a large extent with clinical psychology, and the boundary between the two fields is somewhat blurred. In the United States, the majority of counselling psychologists are employed in student counselling services in secondary schools, universities, and colleges. In Britain, universities, polytechnics, and colleges employ counselling psychologists on a smaller scale, and educational psychologists often perform counselling functions in schools. Other major employers of counselling psychologists in the United States include large commercial and industrial companies, government agencies, and the armed services, but opportunities for counselling psychologists in these settings remain comparatively restricted in other countries. A growing number of psychologists in the United States, Britain, and elsewhere are employed by specialist counselling agencies, such as marriage guidance councils.

Student counselling, particularly in the United States, is still devoted largely to educational and vocational guidance. Much of this work involves providing students with factual information about educational and training courses and careers, and such mundane matters as student accommodation. A related area of work involves helping students to plan their future careers. For this purpose, considerable use is made of standardized psychological tests of abilities, aptitudes, scholastic achievement, interests, and personality traits. Assessment work of this kind overlaps with some of the activities of personnel psychologists (see below). A final important aspect of the work of a student counsellor is devoted to therapeutic counselling of students with emotional, interpersonal, or work problems. In this field of activity, counselling psychology resembles clinical psychology, and similar techniques are used. But in general the problems which are dealt with, distressing though they may be, are of a transient and non-clinical nature. Severe psychological disorders, when they are encountered by student counsellors, are usually referred to psychiatrists or clinical psychologists.

Community psychology emerged as a semi-independent field of applied psychology in the 1960s and 1970s out of a disenchantment among some people with traditional approaches to psychological disorders. It has developed on a fairly large scale in the United States, where psychologists working in this area are employed in community mental health centres, welfare agencies, and family counselling services.

The distinguishing features of community psychology are that psychological problems are tackled at a community rather than an individual level, and that the goal is prevention rather than treatment. In contrast to clinical psychologists, who deal only with people who actively seek help or with patients in hospitals and clinics, community psychologists work directly in the community trying to create conditions which favour mental health and well-being. Certain conditions of housing, education, child-rearing, and employment are known to be associated with the emergence of psychological problems; community psychologists try to prevent these conditions from arising, or to ameliorate their effects in communities where they are known to exist. They devote special attention to certain sections of the community, such as ethnic minorities, economically deprived groups, the aged, delinquents, prisoners, alcoholics, and drug addicts, and play a part in establishing and administering various forms of 'crisis intervention' through 24-hour suicide prevention telephone services and the like. Their activities are closely linked with those of social workers and, to a lesser extent, urban planners, public administrators, and civic authorities.

Educational Psychology

In Britain and several other parts of the world, educational psychology is one of the largest and most active fields of applied psychology. In the United States, the term 'educational psychology' is sometimes reserved for certain aspects of psychology which are included in teacher training courses or investigated in educational research organizations, and professional educational psychologists are normally called 'school psychologists'. School psychologists in the United States are employed directly by individual schools or school systems; educational psychologists in Britain are employed by local education authorities, and they work chiefly in child guidance clinics or school psychological services.

Professional careers in educational psychology involve working directly with children of all ages, investigating emotional, behavioural, and learning problems, and making recommendations with regard to remedial treatment. A considerable amount of time is spent consulting with teachers and parents, and with social workers, medical doctors, and others who may be professionally involved with individual children. The kinds of problems frequently encountered include poor eyesight or hearing; psychological and emotional disorders such as childhood autism and test anxiety; truancy and school phobia; specific learning disabilities, most often in the areas of language, reading, or arithmetic; social and personality problems; and children 'at risk' in violent or disturbed family environments. Children are often referred to professional educational psychologists by teachers and parents on account of poor scholastic achievement, particularly when this is thought to have causes other than lack of ability. Others are referred because of disruptive behaviour in school, or other forms of behaviour which teachers or parents regard as undesirable or abnormal.

One of the main functions of a professional educational psychologist is the psychological assessment of children and the diagnosis of problems. If a child is performing poorly in school, for example, it may be necessary to decide whether this is attributable to generalized mental handicap, emotional disturbance, social or interpersonal problems involving teachers or other children in the school, problems in the home environment, severe psychological disorder of some kind, or simply poor eyesight. The child's teachers and parents may have strong views about the source of the problem, and the child may also offer some explanation, but the cause of the problem may transpire on careful investigation to be quite different from any of these suggestions. As an aid to assessment and diagnosis, professional educational psychologists often make use of psychometric tests specifically designed to provide answers to questions of this kind, in addition to informal interviews with the children who are referred to them. Other sources of information which are frequently used include school records, and interviews with teachers, parents, and social workers. In some cases, it is considered necessary to observe a child in the home environment.

A different area of work in which professional educational psychologists are often involved is devoted to individual group therapy or counselling with children or whole families. Long term therapy is seldom necessary since most of the problems which are encountered in practice are relatively minor. Severe psychological problems, when they are found, are usually referred to psychiatrists, paediatricians, speech therapists, and other specialists. Children who are judged to suffer from severe mental handicap or psychological disorders may be transferred, on the recommendation of professional educational psychologists, to special schools or child psychiatric units. Problems which fall directly within the area of expertise of professional educational psychologists may, however, be dealt with on a long-term basis without referral. Work in this area overlaps with clinical and counselling psychology, but demands specialized skills in dealing with children and particular knowledge of problems related to educational adjustment.

On account of their special skills and training, professional educational psychologists are uniquely qualified to perform evaluation research. They are often called upon to evaluate the effectiveness of educational policies and teaching programmes which are instituted in individual schools or school systems. A school which has been running a remedial reading programme for a period of time may, for example, call upon the methodological, statistical, and assessment skills of a professional educational psychologist to reach a verdict on whether or not the programme is achieving its intended goals, and to offer recommendations on how the programme might be improved.

There are a number of controversies within the profession of educational psychology which are worth mentioning. The first revolves around access to records: some professional educational psychologists consider their records to be confidential, while others believe that teachers, parents, and even the children to whom they relate (if they are old enough) ought to be given access to them. The second controversy relates to the question of labelling. Some professional educational psychologists see it as one of their chief functions to give appropriate names to the problems which they diagnose, while others are concerned to avoid labelling, which they believe has negative effects of various kinds on certain children. The third controversy arises from the question: 'Who are the clients?'. While some professional educational psychologists consider the children with whom they work to be their clients, others view themselves as working primarily on behalf of schoolteachers or parents, since it is they who typically refer children for assessment and remedial treatment.

Industrial, Environmental and Organizational Psychology

The fields of applied psychology which are outlined in this section include those which are usually referred to in Britain as *occupational psychology*, namely personnel and engineering psychology, as well as environmental, consumer, and organizational psychology. Most of the psychologists who pursue professional careers in these fields are either in government service or working for commercial and industrial companies in the private sector. The British government employs psychologists chiefly in the Department of Employment and the Manpower Services Commission, the Ministry of Defence, the Civil Service Department, and the Department of the Environment. A certain number are employed in the Prison Service, where work falling into the area of occupational psychology forms part of their activities. In the United States, a wider range of opportunities for industrial, environmental, and organizational psychologists is available in government service, and a larger proportion are employed by private companies than in Britain.

Personnel psychology is devoted largely to job analysis,

personnel selection and placement, and training of workers in industry. In order to perform a job analysis, a psychologist usually begins by producing a job description, which is a detailed account of the work normally done by a person carrying out the job in question. The next step is to construct a job specification, which describes what a person performing the job ought ideally to do. The psychologist is then in a position to draw up a set of job requirements, which detail the skills and training required for a person to perform the work satisfactorily. The set of job requirements may be thought of as a distilled analysis of the personal factors which are important in carrying out the work. Job analyses are used in almost all branches of personnel research and administration, including the selection and placement of workers in particular jobs, and the estimation of worker productivity for purposes of promotion. They serve as useful guides to recruiters, they provide the basis upon which screening tests for applicants are constructed, and they are of use to instructors in specifying the skills which need to be developed in training employees for particular jobs.

Most personnel psychologists spend a great deal of their working time on personnel selection and placement; it is obviously in the interests of both employers and employees that people should be recruited into jobs which are most suited to their individual attributes. Personnel selection and placement became firmly established during the Second World War, when work in the United States and the British Commonwealth showed that carefully constructed paper-and-pencil tests and psychomotor examinations could successfully identify people most likely to succeed at complex jobs, such as those of aircraft pilots, navigators, and bombardiers.

One class of tests which are widely used by personnel psychologists are those devoted to specific aptitudes and abilities. Research has suggested that five groups of aptitudes and abilities are particularly important in the sense that they account, singly or in various combinations, for success in a wide range of jobs. They are the following: verbal ability, spatial visualization, numerical ability, perceptual speed and accuracy, and psychomotor ability (which includes manual dexterity). Reliable and valid tests have been devised for measuring these aptitudes and abilities, and they are widely used by personnel psychologists. Equally useful for certain kinds of jobs are tests of interests and personality, since research has shown that these can be evaluated more accurately by properly constructed objective tests than by informal methods such as interviews.

When test results, together with other information such as employment records and references, are used for purposes of selecting personnel and placing them in suitable positions, various factors have to be borne in mind. One important factor is the relative seriousness of two different kinds of selection or placement errors. In selecting astronauts, for example, the consequences of false positives (incorrect predictions that particular candidates will succeed at the job) are likely to be much more costly than false negatives (incorrect predictions that particular candidates will turn out to be unsuitable). In selecting trainee computer programmers, on the other hand, false positives may not be considered a serious problem, and the primary goal may be to avoid overlooking potentially able candidates, ie to avoid false negatives.

Personnel psychologists are sometimes involved in devising and evaluating methods of training employees for particular jobs. A large number of training procedures are available, including on-the-job coaching, demonstrations, simulations (widely used for training pilots of large aircraft), lectures, printed instruction manuals, films, and programmed or computer-administered instruction. The optimal combination of training methods for a particular job depends upon considerations of time, expense, and effectiveness, and personnel psychologists are frequently required to weigh these factors up in deciding upon the method or methods to be used in specific cases.

Engineering psychology, which in Europe is often called *ergonomics*, differs from personnel psychology in so far as it is concerned with fitting jobs to people rather than with fitting people to jobs. Engineering psychologists or ergonomists spend their time designing jobs, equipment, and work places in such a way that performance and well-being are maximized, while accidents, fatigue, boredom, and energy expenditure are minimized. *Environmental psychology* shares many of the methods and concerns of engineering psychology, but it focusses on aspects of the built and natural environment outside the work situation. Both of these fields of applied psychology rest heavily on the findings of pure experimental research. In particular, research findings in the areas of sensation, perception, learning, memory, and attention (see Chapter 3) have important implications for engineering and environmental psychology.

One of the most important activities of engineering psychologists is devoted to equipment design. With the development during the Second World War of extremely complex machines controlled by human operators, such as advanced military aircraft, methods of designing optimal man-machine systems gradually evolved. Early work on equipment design centred on finding the best ways of arranging controls and instrument panels. This type of 'knobs and dials' psychology led to significant improvements in equipment design. One type of improvement, for example, arose from the discovery of a host of 'population stereotypes' with respect to the ways in which people (often unconsciously) expect controls to function. A simple instance is the following: most people expect a knob to produce an increase in electrical output when it is turned clockwise, and a decrease when it is turned anticlockwise; but a water or gas tap is usually expected to function in exactly the opposite way: clockwise turning is expected to decrease the flow, and anticlockwise turning to increase it. Engineering psychologists now know a great deal about how to design equipment so as to make work efficient and comfortable, and environmental psychologists have extended this type of concern to aspects of the design of buildings and living spaces.

Engineering psychologists devote a great deal of attention to the effects on human performance of such things as fatigue, boredom, and noise. As industrial processes become more and more automated, an increasing number of jobs require continued alertness or vigilance over long periods of time. In monitoring tasks, for example, a worker may be required to pay continuous attention to a computer display and to respond quickly to particular kinds of signals. Research in the area of human performance has produced many important findings which are applied in designing jobs of this kind.

The British Postal Code (the equivalent of the American Zip Code) may be used to illustrate the way in which pure experimental research is applied by engineering psychologists to familiar problems. The following findings have emerged from the laboratories of experimental psychologists: (a) strings of letters or digits can be copied and remembered more quickly and accurately if they are presented in groups of three than in any other way; (b) digits are easier to copy and remember than letters; (c) items in the middle of strings are more likely to be copied or recalled inaccurately than those at the beginnings and ends. On the recommendations of engineering psychologists, these findings were used in the design of the British Postal Code as follows. Six characters, in two groups of three, are used. They are not all digits, since this would provide only a million combinations, which is too few for the number of addresses in the country. On the other hand, six letters would provide more combinations than are necessary. So the

British Postal Code uses four letters and two digits, and the digits are placed in the middle of the string where errors are

most likely. The Postal Code of the British Psychological Society, for example, is LE1 7DR. The result is a system which maximizes the speed and accuracy of addressing and sorting mail. (Any personal evidence which may seem to contradict this should not shake the reader's faith in engineering psychology!)

Consumer psychology is concerned with problems of advertizing and selling, and with the investigation of consumer attitudes and behaviour as an aid to designing better (or, in most cases, more profitable) products and services. Many of its theories and methods are drawn from the area of social psychology (see Chapter 3). Contemporary consumer psychologists are sometimes concerned with the uses which people make of products after purchasing them, and some, particularly in the United States, provide technical services and carry out research for consumer organizations and government agencies with a view to formulating and implementing consumer protection measures. The majority of consumer psychologists are, however, employed by private companies and advertizing or market research organizations. Their two major activities are testing advertizing effectiveness and carrying out market research.

Testing the effectiveness of advertisements is a notoriously difficult task. It is seldom possible to judge the impact of an advertisement or an advertizing campaign by simply examining sales figures. The reason for this is that there are usually too many confounding factors which are likely to influence sales, including advertisements for competing products. In any event, since advertisements are often extremely expensive, organizations are often anxious to test them in other ways. Numerous sophisticated techniques have been developed by consumer psychologists for performing such tests, although some experts in the field are sceptical about their usefulness.

The second major activity of consumer psychologists is carrying out market research. Work in this area involves surveying the attitudes of specified groups of consumers or potential consumers of particular products or services and the uses which they make of these products or services. The results of surveys of this kind are used in designing products, packages, and advertizing campaigns, and in choosing trade names. In conducting market surveys, one of the most important problems is the choice of suitable methods of sampling. This problem arises, of course, in all kinds of survey research, and special techniques have been devised for handling it. Another major problem is the construction of reliable and valid questionnaires and other types of scales for measuring attitudes. Both these problems were discussed in Chapter 3.

An instructive example of the kind of unexpected and useful information which can emerge from market research is found in the history of the paper handkerchief. This product was originally marketed by Kleenex as a facial tissue for removing cleansing cream. Market research revealed, however, that many women were using Kleenex tissues as handkerchiefs. This finding led to a completely new approach to marketing the product, in which its advantages over the conventional linen handkerchief were emphasized and the potential market was recognized to include not only women but also children and men.

Organizational psychology focusses on the structure and functioning of organizations and the activities of people within them. Although it has been devoted chiefly to industrial organizations, it is being increasingly often applied in hospitals, schools, prisons, military units, and other non-industrial organizations. This branch of applied psychology draws heavily on research in the areas of individual differences and personality, and social psychology (see Chapter 3).

An important part of organizational psychology is devoted to studying the effect of various leadership styles adopted by supervisors on organizational productivity or effectiveness. Some supervisors habitually adopt task-oriented directive-managerial styles of leadership, while others use more human-relations-oriented non-directive styles. A great deal of applied research has been carried out in an effort to discover how effective these leadership styles are in various organizational settings. The work of the American psychologist Fred Fiedler has been particularly influential in this area in recent times. According to Fiedler's theory, directive-managerial leadership is most effective in situations which are either extremely favourable or extremely unfavourable from the point of view of the supervisor; non-directive leadership, on the other hand, is most effective in situations of intermediate favourableness. The favourableness of the situation depends upon such factors as the friendliness of the supervisor-worker relations, the amount of power invested in the supervisor's role position in the organization, and the degree of structure in the tasks which the workers have to perform. If, for example, supervisor-worker relations are good, the supervisor has a powerful position, and the work is highly structured, then the situation is highly favourable for the supervisor, and Fiedler's theory predicts that directive-managerial leadership will prove most effective. The same applies if the situation is unfavourable on all three dimensions. But in situations of intermediate favourableness, non-directive leadership is held to be most effective. Fiedler's theory has been tested in various types of organizations and the results have been generally supportive. The theory has obvious and important implications for the assignment of particular supervisors to suitable positions in organizations, and it is widely used by organizational psychologists.

Another important part of organizational psychology concerns questions of job satisfaction, employee attitudes and motivation, and their effects on absenteeism, labour turnover, and organizational productivity or effectiveness. Evidence from applied research in this area has revealed that job satisfaction depends largely upon the relationship between employee expectations and experience on the job. When experience in a job fails to live up to expectations, job satisfaction tends to be low, although the same work might produce quite high levels of job satisfaction among employees whose expectations are appropriate to the nature of the job. This suggests that it is in the interests of management to ensure that prospective employees are given realistic information about jobs rather than being misled into expecting more than the jobs can offer.

Numerous investigations have shown that low job satisfaction leads to high absenteeism and labour turnover, but there is no simple relationship between job satisfaction and productivity. The most important factors which, when weighed in relation to expectations, determine job satisfaction appear to be the nature of the work itself, wages or salaries, attitudes towards supervisors, relations with co-workers, and opportunities for promotion. A scale known as the *Job Descriptive Index* is widely used by organizational psychologists for measuring job satisfaction in these five areas when, for example, investigating the causes of high rates of absenteeism or labour turnover in an organization.

How to Become a Psychologist

Having absorbed the material presented in earlier sections of this book, the reader should have a reasonably sound knowledge of the nature and subject matter of psychology, its aims, methods, and historical development, and the range of career opportunities available to properly qualified psychologists. Some readers will no doubt have come to the conclusion that psychology is definitely not for them, although they may have thought about becoming psychologists before reading this book; their misconceptions have been corrected in a relatively inexpensive and painless way. A second class of readers may be sufficiently attracted by psychology to wish to read more deeply into the subject, and the background provided by this book will help them to find their bearings in more specialized psychological literature. A third class of readers may seriously consider becoming qualified and possibly pursuing professional careers in psychology. A few comments about qualifications and training may therefore be helpful.

The first step on the road to becoming a qualified psychologist is the satisfactory completion of secondary schooling. The basic qualification for all careers in psychology is a recognized first degree, and admission into degree courses usually depends upon secondary school examination results. In Britain, for example, the minimum requirements normally include two A-level passes and, in some cases, mathematics at O-level; but competition for places on undergraduate courses is quite intense and bare passes are usually insufficient to ensure admission. (The formal requirements are, however, sometimes waived for mature applicants.) Competition for places on joint or combined degree courses, in which psychology is read in conjunction with one or more other subjects, is sometimes less severe than for single subject courses, and some (but not all) joint and combined honours degrees are recognized by the British Psychological Society as conferring eligibility for Graduate Membership, which is a necessary prerequisite for entry into most postgraduate professional training courses. Conversion courses are available at some institutions for graduates in subjects other than psychology, and eligibility for Graduate Membership can be acquired by passing the British Psychological Society's Qualifying Examination. Suitable school subjects for intending psychology students include psychology, biology, mathematics, and English, but most degree course selectors are more concerned with grades than with the subjects in which they are obtained. In the United States, the criteria for admission into degree courses vary considerably, and competition at this level is usually less intense than in Britain.

During the three or four years of study towards a first degree, a student is expected to master the basic concepts, theories, and findings in all the major areas of psychology, and to acquire elementary statistical and research skills. The range of topics covered in undergraduate syllabuses comes as something of a surprise to many students, but readers of this book will have a fairly good idea of what to expect. Methods of teaching may include lectures, tutorials, seminars, and laboratory classes, and towards the end of their courses students are often expected to carry out small-scale research projects. Assessment procedures vary from one institution to the next, but are usually based upon a combination of examination results and marks obtained for projects, laboratory reports, and essays during the course.

A first degree does not, on its own, qualify a person to practise in all fields of psychology. In the United States, very few careers in psychology are open to first degree graduates. In Britain, first degree graduates may apply for psychology teaching posts in colleges, and for jobs as occupational, consumer, and prison psychologists, in which further training takes place on the job. Higher degrees are, however, very helpful in gaining employment in these fields. For other careers, a further qualification is virtually essential. In most countries, including Britain, entry into postgraduate training courses is highly competitive, and depends largely upon results obtained in first degrees. In the United States, applicants for places on postgraduate programmes are often required to take entrance examinations.

In order to practise as a clinical psychologist in the National Health Service, a psychologist in Britain must possess a first degree recognized by the British Psychological Society, and then either (a) complete a two-year postgraduate professional training course at a university or a teaching hospital, or (b) complete three years' in-service training as a probationer clinical psychologist and then pass the British Psychological Society's Diploma Examination in Clinical Psychology. An educational psychologist in Britain must complete a recognized first degree in psychology, and then obtain a Postgraduate Certificate in Education and accumulate two years' teaching experience, and finally complete a one-year professional training course in educational psychology. Psychology teachers in schools are normally expected to possess recognized teaching qualifications, and applications for teaching posts in higher and further education are usually evaluated according to their formal qualifications (usually including higher degrees), publications, and teaching experience. Qualifications for other psychological careers in Britain are less clearly defined, but normally require postgraduate qualifications such as masters or doctoral degrees.

In the United States, the qualifications for teaching posts in psychology are not formally specified, but higher degrees are usually essential in practice. In most states, however, work in any area of applied psychology requires certification or licensing. In order to become certified or licensed, a psychologist must normally have been awarded the degree of PhD in psychology by a recognized university (this takes an average of five years study after completing a first degree), have accumulated two years' supervised experience, and have passed a qualifying examination. The qualifying examination is in most cases a standard multiple-choice test of the candidate's knowledge in all major fields of psychology rather than in his or her own specialism, and the license or certificate allows the psychologist to practise in any applied field. The highest level of accreditation — which is not legally required in order to practise — is given by the American Board of Professional Psychology (ABPP), originally set up by the American Psychological Association. This body confers separate diplomas in clinical, counselling, industrial and organizational, and school psychology Before taking an examination for one of these advanced diplomas, a candidate must possess a recognized PhD degree in psychology, and have a minimum of five years' professional experience in one of the four areas of applied psychology in which the diplomas are available.

Further Reading

One of the most comprehensive and up-to-date surveys of applied psychology is Ann Anastasi's *Fields of Applied Psychology*, 2nd ed. (New York: McGraw-Hill, 1980). The American Psychological Association (1200 17th Street, N.W., Washington DC 20036) has published a great deal of information about careers, and a free pamphlet entitled *Careers in Psychology* can be obtained by writing directly to the Association. The British Psychological Society (St Andrews House, 48 Princess Road East, Leicester LE1 7DR) also supplies a free pamphlet on *Careers in Psychology*, as well as separate pamphlets on careers in clinical, educational, occupational, prison, and social psychology. A useful guide to British first degree courses in psychology can be obtained from the Careers Research and Advisory Centre (Bateman Street, Cambridge CB2 1LZ).

Index